STO

FRIENDS
OF ACPL

Nothing Rhymes with April

NAOMI J. KARP

Nothing Rhymes with April

Illustrated by Pamela Johnson

HARCOURT BRACE JOVANOVICH
NEW YORK AND LONDON

Text copyright © 1974 by Naomi J. Karp
Illustrations copyright © 1974
by Harcourt Brace Jovanovich, Inc.
All rights reserved.
No part of this publication may be reproduced
or transmitted in any form or by any means,
electronic or mechanical, including photocopy, recording,
or any information storage and retrieval system,
without permission in writing from the publisher.
Printed in the United States of America
First edition
B C D E F G H I J K

Library of Congress Cataloging in Publication Data
Karp, Naomi J
 Nothing rhymes with April.
 SUMMARY: An eleven-year-old girl growing up during the Depression learns the meaning of the word "dignity" through the experiences of the people around her.
 [1. Depression—1929—Fiction] I. Johnson, Pamela, illus. II. Title.
PZ7.K148No   [Fic]   73-17938
ISBN 0-15-257579-0

1800083

*For Mom, Dad, Marty, Betsy,
Leslie, Jon, Jeff, and Ace*

Nothing Rhymes with April

CHAPTER *One*

As she approached Higgins' Toy Shop, Mollie closed her eyes. "Oh, please be there, please, please," she said softly to herself. "I won't look. I'll keep my eyes tight shut until I get past Higgins' window." That would take about twelve steps, she figured.
Clutching her schoolbag to her stomach, she counted the steps. There, twelve. Safe! She opened her left eye, then her right, expecting to see the window of the Star Bakery, the store just beyond Higgins'.
"Phooey!" she said aloud, for there before her eyes, the sunlight turning the rust to an orangey gold, was the bicycle.
"I should've taken longer steps," she thought, staring at the store window. For the hundredth time, she examined the bent spokes of the wheels, the piece of torn leather hanging from the seat, the six letters on the crossbar that was all that was left of the name: IV JO BI.
"I wonder why nobody has bought it. It's so perfect," she asked herself, also for the hundredth time. But she knew the answer. Who could afford it—even though it cost only seven dollars second-hand?
At least, that's what her father had told her when she had mentioned the bicycle the first time. "We are living

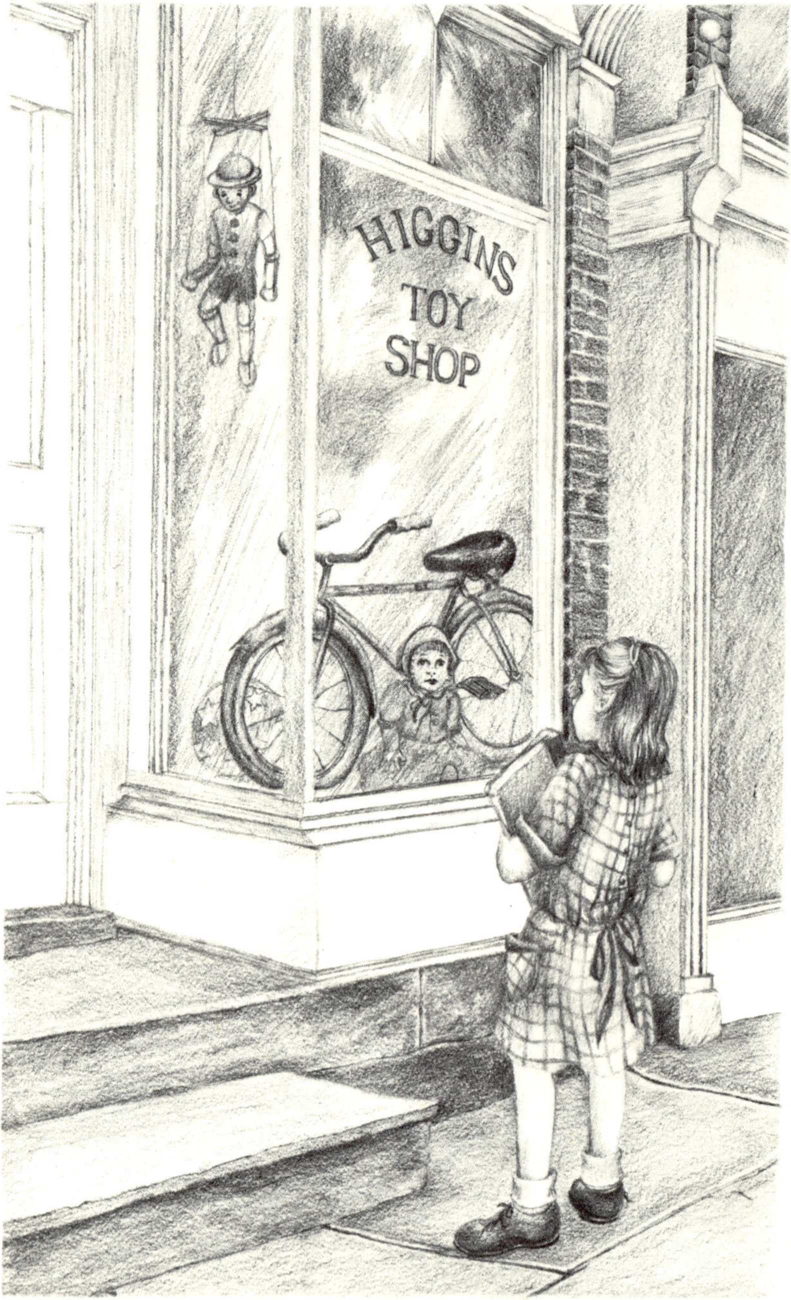
HIGGINS
TOY
SHOP

through a Depression, Mollie. Do you realize that a bicycle is a luxury?"

"I thought a luxury was eating out in a restaurant. That's what Mom says," she told her father.

"That's one luxury, and a bicycle is another. You have two strong legs. They can carry you wherever you want to go, and for nothing," her father had told her gently.

Mollie hadn't argued. She knew if her father was able to buy the bicycle, he surely would. He would do anything for her because she was his favorite. Not that he ever said so—he didn't talk very much about such things—but Mollie just knew.

She gave one final look at the bike in Higgins' window and started home.

"Oh, rusty-fendered bicycle
As shining as an icicle,
Please wait for me until I'm rich.
I'll never ride you in a ditch."

Mollie recited to herself as she walked home. That was as far as she had gotten on her "Ode to a Rusty Bike." She had written it carefully in her secret notebook, which she named *The Golden Poems of Mollie Stone*. Actually, there was no reason to call them golden—the notebook was black—except that it sounded nice.

This was her seventh poem in the book. The first, her very first, was her favorite.

"House of brick, house of fire,
Bringing me my heart's desire.
Sunlight on the windowpane,
Roof protecting all from rain."

She wondered if she would ever again write one as beautiful.

"Oh boy, are you gonna get it," her brother called from the kitchen as Mollie opened the front door. "Mom said you had to be home to take care of me when I got home and you weren't, and I'm gonna tell and you're gonna get it."

His big blue eyes sparkled with happiness at the thought of Mollie's "getting it." Danny was seven, four years younger than Mollie, and probably the world's greatest tattletale. His favorite victim was his sister, but he had been known to tattle on perfect strangers—like the man who accidentally knocked over a can of peas in the grocery store or the baby who had thrown his rattle into a rosebush.

Mollie ignored him. Usually her parents ignored his tattling, too. He told so many stories that nobody ever listened. When Danny reported that Mollie had pushed him on the stairs or refused to lend him her skate key, Mr. Stone would nod and say, "That's nice!" and go right on reading or working on his papers.

Danny was finishing a jelly sandwich at the kitchen table. His eyes followed Mollie as she opened the cupboard, took out some graham crackers, and ate them.

"Crumbs, you're dropping crumbs!" he shouted happily. "I'm gonna tell."

Mollie scattered the crumbs with the toe of her shoe.

"Another thing I'm gonna tell is that I was right behind you on the way home and I saw you lookin' in Higgins' window."

"Really? I thought you were home before me and were waiting for me to take care of you." Mollie stuck her tongue out at Danny.

"I came through the Weller's backyard. Ha ha."

Mollie shrugged her shoulders and bit into another cracker.

" 'Oh, rusty-fendered bicycle . . .' " Danny began.

Mollie's eyes narrowed. "You couldn't have heard me, you little. . . . Have you been sneaking into my notebook?" she shouted, raising her arm.

"If you hit me, I'm gonna tell," Danny shouted back, and scooted behind her out the back door.

Mollie considered chasing him and knocking his head against a tree, but he was so slippery and small that she could never catch him. Instead, she ran upstairs to her room where *The Golden Poems of Mollie Stone* were hidden between her red and blue sweaters in the dresser drawer. The notebook was there, but the sweaters were rumpled as if someone had put them back in a hurry.

With great care, she picked up the notebook and turned the pages. Everything was in order, except that when she read the lines about the bicycle, she could hear Danny's voice squeaking her precious words. Somehow, the poem had changed—it was no good. She would have to write another and find a new hiding place.

"Oh, rotten little tattletale
I'd like to put you straight in jail
And feed you wormy bread to eat
And tie your mouth and hands and feet
So that my poems you can't repeat."

Mollie giggled. Not bad, she decided as she reread the lines. Danny had given her a good idea for a poem, but he was never going to ride her bike, that little brat. Maybe *she* never would either. Phooey on the Depression! What did it have to do with her, anyway?

At least what she had seen of it last Saturday afternoon at the movies had nothing to do with her. There it was, just before the new chapter of Flash Gordon's battle with Ming the Merciless on Planet X. As usual, the theater had grown darker, the parade music began, the torn curtain that covered the movie screen opened with a squeak that reminded Mollie of chalk breaking on the school blackboard, and the booming voice began, "Ladies and gentlemen, 'The March of Time.'"

As if this were some sort of signal, all the boys in the audience began to throw bubble gum at each other, and all the girls, including Mollie, said, "Sh-sh! Shut up! Be quiet!"

Mollie liked this part of the program almost as much as the Flash Gordon serial, the cartoons, and the two movies that followed. It told about all the things that happened in the world that week. Some Saturdays there were kings and queens shaking hands, or ladies in fur coats waving from the decks of big ocean liners. Almost every week they showed soldiers in stiff uniforms marching without bending their knees and holding their right arms straight in front of them. But last Saturday they showed the Depression, and Mollie could see it had nothing to do with her.

The Depression was skinny men who needed shaves waiting in long lines for a cup of soup from the Salvation Army or for a job in an old brick factory with dirty windows.

"More than four hundred men lined up at these factory gates before dawn last Monday after hearing that there might be work available," The March of Time announcer explained. "Most have been unemployed since the stock market crashed seven years ago. Some of the men had walked fifty miles to reach the factory, and there was a near riot when they discovered the factory had been shut down for several months."

Then the newsreel had shown farmers in patched overalls staring at their empty fields while their children, with blond, stringy hair and big, sad eyes, huddled together on the porches of broken-down farmhouses.

"There is little relief from the Depression for these families," the booming voice continued. "With no money for seed, these farmers will once again have no crops. And the soil, once rich and fertile, is now dry, windswept dust."

Mollie had felt sad when she saw this. She pretended to be one of the blond, sad children and sat huddled in the smooth seat of the movie house, sniffing softly and making believe she was crying about the dusty, empty farms.

But by the time the matinee had ended, she had forgotten all about the Depression until this afternoon—when she had again seen her beloved bike in Higgins' window and realized, even though she did not have blond hair and sad eyes and her father did not need a shave, that she could not have it because of the Depression.

That night, at the dinner table, Mollie told her parents about the newsreel she had seen on Saturday.

"The March of Time said that there's a Depression because something crashed. The announcer said it happened at the market and lots of men have no jobs. I don't know which market, do you, Dad?"

"It was the A & P," Mollie's brother squeaked. "I saw a lady drop a whole bottle of milk. I told the man . . ."

"It was the stock market," Mollie's father interrupted, "in 1929. That was seven years ago . . ."

"Seven years? I'm seven years, too," Danny squeaked again.

"Please, Danny," Mr. Stone said firmly. "I'm trying to explain something very difficult to Mollie."

"Nyaah," Mollie snickered at her brother, and Mrs. Stone, who was starting to clear the table, said he could go out and play.

"Seven years ago," her father began again, "on a day in October they call Black Friday, the stock market crashed. Now don't *you* interrupt me also. Let me explain.

"In the 1920's, even before you were born, Mollie, the country began to grow bigger and richer. There were lots of new businesses, and people began to make more money than they ever thought they could. Many people put their money in banks. A great many others started businesses of their own or invested in . . ."

"What's 'invested in' mean?" Mollie asked.

"It means they gave money to somebody else's company so that the company could grow and make more products."

"But why would they give it away?"

"Well, they didn't exactly give it away. They bought a part of the business with it. This is called buying stock in a company. And when the company made more money, they gave part of it back to the investors. They did all this through the Stock Exchange, a place that handled the money for the investors and for the companies."

"But what about the Depression?" Mollie asked again.

"Well, it reached a point where most people thought that owning stock was the most important thing in the world. They borrowed money to buy stock; they didn't care how much the stock cost or whether the company they were investing in was making money. Why, a stock that the first investor paid ten dollars for, he could soon sell for twenty, and the fellow who bought it for twenty could sell it for fifty. The whole country went crazy buying, buying, buying."

"Did you buy stock, too?" Mollie asked her father.

"Oh, yes. I was no different." He smiled a funny smile and looked at Mollie's mother. Mrs. Stone shook her head and smiled, too.

"O.K., what happened then?" Mollie asked. If her father talked long enough, the kitchen would soon be cleaned up.

"After a while, some smart people began to see that the stock prices were too high. They decided to sell their stock instead of buying it. And then more people began to get nervous and sell *their* stock. And when lots of people are selling the same thing, what happens?"

"I . . . it . . . I don't know. What happens?"

"The prices go down," her father explained.

"But that was good, wasn't it?"

"No, that was bad. Because the prices went down so far that soon the stock wasn't worth anything and people lost all their money."

"Was that the crash?" Mollie guessed.

"That was indeed the crash."

"But you told me before that some people put their

16

money in banks instead of stocks. Weren't they still rich?"

"If they got to the banks soon enough," her father said, "because very soon after the crash, the banks ran out of money."

"Can you imagine, Mollie, how terrible it was?" her mother said, giving the countertop a last wipe with the dishcloth. "Some people who worked all their lives and saved their money in banks went to the banks and were told, 'Sorry, there is no more money left. We gave it all away yesterday.'"

"Were you one of those people?" Mollie asked. Now she was sorry she hadn't helped her mother with the dishes.

"No, but some of Daddy's clients were," her mother explained. "That's why they can't always pay him when he does work for them." Mrs. Stone glanced at her husband, and he shook his head as if to say, "Let's not go into that now."

But Mollie had heard her parents talk about that many times before. About how her father, who was a lawyer, did lots of work for people, helping them when they lost their businesses, going to court, and looking over lots of papers. They had no money to pay him, they said, but they did have some merchandise left over from their businesses. Couldn't they give him some of this and a little of that until they got back on their feet?

So Mr. Stone would come home some nights with a case of silk scarves or forty leather notebooks.

Her father had said she could have one, and that was now *The Golden Poems of Mollie Stone*.

"Well, why didn't they have people like us in The March of Time?" Mollie asked. "If we're part of the Depression, too, I mean?"

"The movie screen isn't big enough," her father said with a laugh. "There are many more people like us who can just about manage."

"Really, Mollie, you aren't comparing yourself to those poor little farm children, are you?" Mrs. Stone asked. "You have food in your stomach and a roof over your head."

"But I don't have a bike," Mollie mumbled, although she was glad her parents hadn't heard her, or at least they pretended not to have heard her.

CHAPTER *Two*

" 'A bowl of oatmeal, fair maiden,' the warder cried,
And when she served him, he upped and died."

Not too bad, Mollie thought, gazing into her bowl of hot cereal that was now lumpy from having cooked too long. She liked the word warder—it sounded brave and kind. She was sorry he had to die, but that was the only rhyme she could think of in a hurry. Breakfast was not the best time for creating poetry.

Heavy footsteps sounded on the back porch, followed by a quiet tap at the door.

"Come in, Shell. I'm just getting my books," Mollie called.

A chubby girl with short brown braids entered, her rubber overshoes clumping with every step. She stood by the door as Mollie gathered up her school books.

"Good-bye, all. I'm off in a cloud of dust," Mollie shouted.

Shelley giggled. "You say that every morning."

"I know. It's sort of my farewell speech."

"To whom?"

"To everybody in the house," Mollie said, not bothering to mention that nobody else was in the house. Every morning Mollie ate her breakfast alone. Her father had long ago left for his office and her mother for her job as a nurse at Community Hospital. Mrs. Stone dropped Danny off at school on her way to work because, her mother said, Mollie was "too irresponsible, always dreaming," to get Danny breakfast and off to school.

She and Shelley walked down the porch steps. "The sun is shining," Mollie said. "Why are you wearing those things on your feet?"

"My mother made me. She says it might snow." Shelley's mother was always hovering over her with an extra sweater or a second piece of fruit. "Just in case," Mrs. Weller said, "my Shelley should be caught in a wind or a snowstorm."

"Snow!" Mollie laughed. "Snow! It's April!" Suddenly she stopped. "Wait a minute. Did you hear that?"

"Hear what?" Shelley looked around fearfully.

"Snow in April. April, April, what rhymes with April? Dapril, Maypril . . . oh, forget it. It must be like orange."

"April is like orange? What are you talking about?"

"Orange. There is absolutely no word in the English language that rhymes with orange. I read that once and it's true."

Shelley looked impressed. Mollie knew so many things, even though she was eleven days younger. On the other hand, Mollie was two inches taller if you counted her thick brown hair that was gathered carelessly on top of her head into a gold barrette.

A sudden sharp sting made Mollie grab her leg. "Ow, I think a bee stung me."

"It's Herbert," Shelley whispered. "He's throwing stones again."

Behind them a skinny boy wearing a baseball cap was just winding up for another pitch.

"Hey, Herbert, you dope, you hit me with a stone," Mollie shouted.

"Well then, take a base," he said. But Herbert was not

really mean, and he turned toward an empty lot for his next throw.

"Honestly," Shelley said, "I'll bet he sleeps in that baseball cap. That's all he talks about. Babe Ruth and home runs."

"I do not," Herbert said, catching up to them. "I talk about, let's see, about. . . . I can give you statistics . . . well, I suppose that's about baseball, too." He thought for a second, apparently surprised at himself.

They had turned the corner and were approaching the square brick school building when Mollie grabbed Shelley's arm. "There they are. I wonder if they got it. Hey, Elaine, hey, Florette, did you get it?"

Florette and Elaine, known as the Songbirds of Laurel Avenue, turned around.

"Did you get it?" Mollie repeated. "The audition, I mean."

"We are still awaiting their call," Florette said, sounding very important. "My mother said not to worry, of course. They are sure to be interested in us."

Mollie and Shelley and even Herbert had heard the Songbirds. Florette, a tall girl with rosy cheeks and badly bitten fingernails, which she occasionally hid in her nostrils, was an alto. The music teacher who came every other Wednesday to teach the classes how to harmonize "Sweet and low, wind of the western sea" had said so.

Elaine, whose long hair hung down her back in giant Tootsie Roll curls, was a soprano. She was allowed to sing solo "Blow them again to me-ee" every other Wednesday.

The girls, or rather their mothers, had decided that Florette and Elaine together made music that the world should be privileged to hear on the radio. Mollie had heard the story from Florette, about how they had written to Uncle Pat's Saturday Morning Children's Hour. They had sent their pictures, both girls dressed alike in white frilly dresses and carrying make-believe fur muffs. Why did they need pictures, Mollie had asked. No one could see them on the radio?

"Oh, one never knows," Florette had told her, sounding just like her mother. "Who knows but what a talent scout may hear us and sign us up for the movies."

Mollie's mother had raised her eyes to the heavens when Mollie repeated the conversation to her. "Who knows? Anybody who hears them knows," she said.

And practically everyone had heard them. They had sung at Mollie's eighth, ninth, and tenth birthday parties and at Shelley's and even at Herbert's, and of course, their own. They even sang "Happy Birthday" to themselves —without being asked.

Mollie often wondered whether the ice cream and cake were worth the price of listening to the Songbirds of Laurel Avenue.

"Be sure to let us know," Mollie called after them just as the first bell rang. "C'mon, we'll be late," she said to Shelley.

"Wouldn't that be something?" Shelley asked. "We'd actually know somebody famous."

"You already know me," Mollie said, only half joking.

"You're cuckoo," Shelley said with a laugh.

CHAPTER *Three*

It was Friday, Mollie realized with a sudden lurch of her heart. All around her were classmates in identical uniforms, the girls wearing white middy blouses with blue scarves tucked beneath the square collars, the boys in white shirts and navy ties.

Mollie, in her red plaid dress, stuck out like an apple on a bedsheet.

"Why didn't my mother remind me?" she thought angrily. Now she would have to march to the assembly hall last in line, behind Philip Sheridan who was six feet tall and at least two hundred pounds. Miss Conklin, the principal, would make her announcements from the stage staring right at her, for where else would her eye be attracted?

Now Miss Felt, the sixth-grade teacher, was staring at her, an attendance sheet in her hand and lips pursed. "Mollie," she said in her pretend British accent, "did you not realize that today is Friday, assembly day, when we all wear our white blouses?" She pronounced it "blowzez."

Mollie thought the word should be "blice" and giggled.

"You think it's amusing? Do you mean to embarrass our entire class by appearing out of Friday uniform?"

"No, I wasn't laughing . . ."

"Never mind. You will march behind the last boy who is . . ." She glanced around the room and pointed with her chin to Philip. "And you will sit on an outside aisle seat so you won't be too obvious."

"Hey, Shortie, just keep your eye on my belt and you won't get lost," Big Philip whispered. He laughed deep in his chest and sounded as if he were belching.

Mollie was miserable. She bit her lip and could feel the anger rise within her own chest. She grabbed a pencil and pretended to be writing the assignment Miss Felt was putting on the blackboard.

> "My dress is red.
> With heart of lead—
> Dear mother forgot to remind me—
> Now I shall march
> With throat so parch
> And nobody behind me."

She felt a little better, but if she mentioned it to her mother, Mollie knew what she would say. "That's your responsibility, my dear. You have so little to think about that the least you could do is remember what day it is." But if she were home in the morning, if she made me breakfast like Shelley's mother, if . . . oh, what was the use. Her mother would probably rejoice in her suffering!

From a distance, Mollie could hear the piano playing the marching-into-assembly tune and the shuffle of the children from the lower grades on their way to the auditorium. Her brother was probably there, walking in his right-size place, wearing a newly ironed white shirt and her father's discarded blue tie, which reached to Danny's knees.

"It's not fair," she said to herself, rising from her seat with everyone else. Songbird Elaine, the shortest, was first in line, Shelley next, and in Mollie's place was Florette, who usually stood behind her. All were out the door when Mollie got into line behind Philip, and he was right—her eyes were just above the level of his belt. He turned and patted her on the head. "C'mon, Shortie," he said.

24

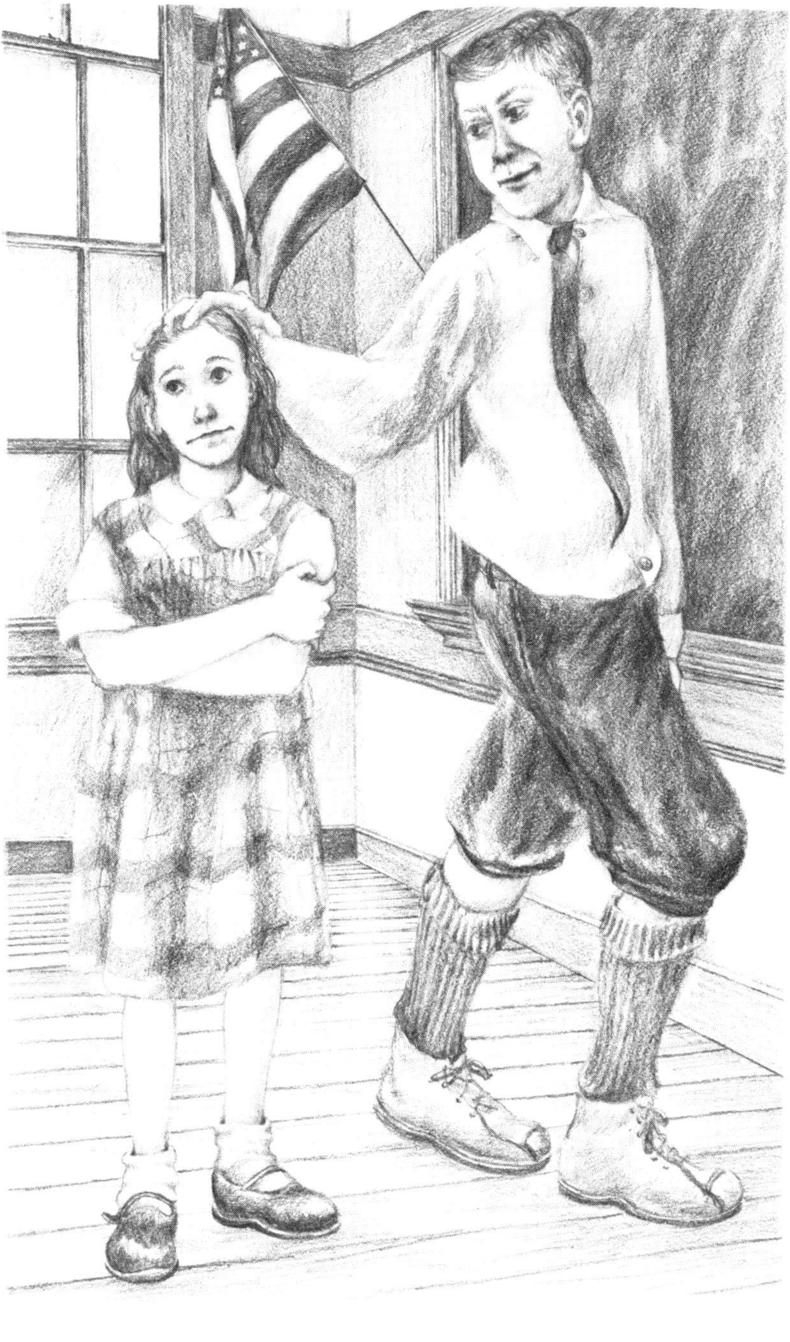

The class walked through the hall, around a corner, and into the many-windowed auditorium where dusty green curtains hung on each side of the stage. There stood Miss Conklin, her eyeglasses reflecting the light and a smile on her face as if she had long been awaiting this excellent group of children.

Mollie liked her and was sorry to ruin the principal's white-bloused assembly with her red dress.

Everyone was seated, the music stopped, and Miss Conklin began speaking in her dry but smiley voice.

"Good morning, children of Public School 132. Will you all rise for a salute to the flag and the singing of the 'Star Spangled Banner.'"

More shuffling noises as everyone rose to a thundering chord of the piano. Mrs. Emmer, the piano player, was also the kindergarten teacher. Mollie had been in her class long ago and knew that Mrs. Emmer never said "Quiet!" or "Sit down!" or "Everyone stand." Instead, she would stand at the tinny piano in the kindergarten room and while facing the children would play that very same chord. It meant quiet, sit down, stand up, or let us sing. A wonderful chord!

The "Star Spangled Banner" ended, and Miss Conklin stepped forward. "Children, I have a most wonderful surprise for you today. Seated in the audience is a special guest. Would you come up here, Mr. Guss?"

A man in a gray suit put his hat down on his seat and walked up the side stairs to the stage.

"This is Mr. Guss. Shall we say, 'How do you do, Mr. Guss'?" She raised one hand like an orchestra leader.

"How do you do, Mr. Guss," the entire assembly said, with the exception of Philip who was one word behind everybody else. His "Mr. Guss" came out all by itself, and he blushed and slumped down in his seat.

"Ha ha," Mollie whispered, glad he was embarrassed.

Mr. Guss did not know whether to look at Miss Conklin

or at the audience, so he looked back and forth like someone watching a ping-pong game.

"Mr. Guss comes to us from the Brotherhood of Atlantis."

Some of the children went "Ooh," although nobody knew what the Brotherhood of Atlantis was.

"This is a most worthy organization," Miss Conklin explained, "of gentlemen who are very interested in . . ." She turned to Mr. Guss for help. He whispered something to her. "Yes, interested in furthering the cause of young talent. But I'll let him explain it himself. Mr. Guss?"

The Brotherhood of Atlantis, Mr. Guss said, in a raspy voice, was holding a contest. This was the third school he had visited this morning, and that's why he was hoarse, he said. There would be a prize for the best short story, the best painting of flowers, and—Mollie held her breath—the best poem about any holiday by public school students. The judges would be the presidents of all the schools' PTA's.

Mollie was so excited that she almost missed the prize announcement. Did she hear it right? Did he say ten dollars for the best, five for second place, and three for third? She asked Philip who was still slumped in his seat.

"Uh," he grunted, shaking his head up and down.

What should she do? Should she submit her favorite poem about house of fire? No, it had to be about a holiday.

"I must win," Mollie thought, forgetting all about her red dress, her embarrassment, and her anger. "I must. I must." For then she would be rich! Ten dollars! Enough to buy the second-hand bike with some left over. "I might even become as famous as the Songbirds," she thought.

CHAPTER *Four*

Her father had come home early that evening. As a matter of fact, she had found him at home when she returned from school. This was very unusual, but she was delighted.

He was bending over the dining room table, arranging some papers in little piles. He had not glanced up when she walked in, even though she had slammed the back door. Mollie put her arms around him and kissed his cheek.

"What are you doing here so early?" she asked.

Finally he looked up at her. "I had an appointment at the bank and didn't want to go back to the office. How's school?" He asked the question as if he were not really interested in her answer.

"O.K." Mollie wanted to tell him about the contest. "Guess what?" she began.

"Mollie!" Danny's voice screeched from the back door. "I told you to wait for me at the side gate. Why didn't you wait for me at the side gate? I had to walk home all by myself, and I'm gonna tell."

Mollie sighed and leaned against the doorway between the dining room and kitchen. "You got home O.K., didn't you? I mean nobody kidnapped you or sold you to the white slavers, right?" Mollie had read about white slavers recently in a newspaper article. It was supposed to sound wicked, but it seemed very romantic to Mollie to be smuggled out of the country and sold to a sultan's harem in some faraway, mysterious land. She had wondered what a harem was and if they took only long-haired girls. Her mother made her have haircuts every two months at Teddy's barbershop where Danny had his hair cut.

"Dad's home," she said. Danny's eyes brightened. Now he would not have to wait to tell anyone of Mollie's forgetfulness. On the other hand, Danny had discovered that telling his father about Mollie was not as much fun as telling his mother. His father only shook his head and looked past him into the distance.

"What time does Mother get home?" Mr. Stone called to Mollie.

"In about an hour."

"Why don't you start dinner for her or set the table?"

"She never lets me cook anything," Mollie said, "except scrambled eggs. You want scrambled eggs?"

"Anything would be nice," her father said, getting back to his papers.

Mollie watched him as he worked. He looked tired, and she could see some gray running through his black hair. Every once in a while he would pick up a paper, examine it, and sigh. She wished she were a very little girl again so she could climb on his lap and feel warm and happy against his soft wool suit and say something to make him laugh.

"Guess what?" she started again, but he did not even turn around.

Mollie went into the kitchen, opened the icebox, and stared into it. There were some eggs, milk, cheese, a few oranges, a loaf of bread, and some meat left over from the day before. She closed the door and went to the cupboard. There were canned vegetables and soup, a box of graham crackers, and a jar of grape jam.

"Tomato soup, scrambled eggs, and for dessert"—she opened the bread box—"cupcakes." It sounded delicious.

She would surprise her mother with dinner all ready, and her father would be very pleased.

She took a can of soup and read the directions on the label. "Easy," Mollie thought. She made a great deal of noise amid the pots and pans, finding one that seemed about the right size. The contents of the can and the added water reached just to the rim. Perfect! She placed the pan on the stove.

Next, the eggs. Mollie cracked the whole dozen into a large mixing bowl, added some milk, a little salt and pepper, and whisked the mixture around with a fork. The fork slipped from her fingers and slid to the bottom of the bowl.

"Ich," Mollie said, putting her hand in to retrieve the fork. She leaned over to wash both her hand and the fork in the sink, and her elbow accidently hit the bowl. It tipped slightly, and some of the yellow mixture spread over the counter.

Mollie scooped it up as best she could with her hand. Behind her there was a sizzling, splattering noise and an awful smell of burning.

"The soup!" she cried, grabbing the handle with her eggy hand. It almost slipped also, and it was hot!

She stared at the burned tomato-soup crust on the stove, noting that it was a very handsome color, like autumn leaves, Mollie thought.

Golden autumn, falling leaves, Mother Nature magic weaves . . .

"My God! What a mess!" Mollie's mother said, rushing into the kitchen. "What have you been doing in here?"

"Making supper. Why?" Mollie looked calmly around the kitchen. Eggs were dripping off the counter, shells were piled in the sink, and the stove was covered with a large brown scab.

"Mollie! How many times have I told you . . . oh, what's the use?" Mrs. Stone began mopping up. "Do you know what you were doing when I came in? Staring at the stove, mumbling to yourself. I really believe you are strange, Mollie. Not only strange, but a slob! How could you make such a mess?" Her mother looked close to tears as she scrubbed the stove. "Do you care that your mother works her fingers to the bone for eight hours a day and then comes home to this?" She held out both hands as if offering the whole messy kitchen to her daughter.

Mr. Stone walked into the kitchen. "It was my fault. I suggested to Mollie . . ."

"Oh, Ben, don't make excuses."

"She was only trying to help, Edith."

"Help?" Mollie's mother shrieked. "Between what you bring home and your daughter's wastefulness, we'll be in the poorhouse."

Mollie's father looked as if he had been slapped across the face.

"Oh, I'm sorry, Ben. I didn't mean that. I know how hard you try and how impossible it is to collect your fees. It's just that I'm so tired."

Mollie took the dishcloth from her mother and wiped the counter. Her heart was beating very fast. A lump was forming in her throat. "Don't cry," she told herself. "Don't let her see you cry!" She clenched her teeth and scrubbed at the sticky counter.

"Don't you think you could at least say you're sorry?" Her mother's voice no longer sounded angry, just weary.

"Why should I?" Mollie mumbled. "I was only trying to help."

"I can't hear you," Mrs. Stone said.

"I said, *I'm sorry*."

Out of the corner of her eye, she could see Danny smiling happily.

CHAPTER *Five*

After the disaster of Mollie's Friday dinner, she decided she would not tell her parents about the poetry contest. Although her father always tried to look interested when she told him about school, she knew he had other things on his mind. It had to do with his law practice, she knew, for she had often heard him discussing it with her mother behind the closed kitchen door.

When this happened, she tried not to listen, but she could not help hearing some of the phrases about "not letting the children worry" or "what will happen next." But while her mother hinted at "hard times," as she had when Mollie ruined the dinner, neither she nor Mr. Stone ever came right out and said, "We are poor; there is no money."

They said merely, "There is not enough money for the bike . . . for a new dress . . . for more meat," which was not the same thing as being like those men in the newsreels or the farmers and their wide-eyed children.

She would never tell her mother, perhaps not even when she won, Mollie decided. Her mother might laugh and tell her she never did anything right, so how did she expect to write a winning poem? No, she would keep it all to herself.

After school during the following week, Mollie ignored Shelley's pleas to come over and play. "My momma just baked some chocolate cake and you can have a big slice," Shelly said temptingly.

"No, I've got something to do," she would say.

"What?"

"I'll tell you someday."

"Why can't you tell me now?" Shelley would ask, and Mollie felt sorry for her friend because lately there had been no one around after school to skip rope or roller skate.

Florette and Elaine were practicing their duet, awaiting the call from Uncle Pat to become famous. Herbert was off with his baseball somewhere, and now Mollie was busy, too.

Shaking loose from Shelley's pleas, Mollie rushed to her room and sat at the small oak desk her parents had bought for her in first grade. She had even refused herself a favorite after-school snack—graham crackers and jam.

"Poets must suffer," she told herself.

Sharpening three pencils with her mother's bread knife, smoothing out the first sheet of blank paper in her notebook, Mollie stared at the ceiling for inspiration.

Holiday, holiday, what would be the best holiday for a poem? Of course, Christmas came to mind first, but Mollie discarded the idea when she could think of nothing but jingle bells.

Thanksgiving? Give thanks for this bounty (whatever bounty was, people were always giving thanks for it).

"Turkey, turkey, gobble good,
Living in his native wood.
Yummy, yummy in my tummy . . ."

Mollie paused for a suitable rhyme, laughed, and wrote, "I think that this poem is crummy."

She would have to do better. She lay down on her bed

and closed her eyes. Something was coming. Mollie jumped off the bed and grabbed a pencil.

"All be merry, gathered here,
Surrounded by folks who are dear,
Saying grace and all good cheer,
Shunning hunger, shunning fear."

Mollie liked the "shunning"; it sounded grown-up, but the poem was not as good on paper as it seemed when she lay with her eyes closed. She examined the end of her pencil and picked up a small calendar, a gift from the Max Morris Insurance Company—"We protect everyone and everything!" She flipped the months watching for those days circled in red, which meant a holiday. Independence Day!

"Washington and Paul Revere
Saying words so loud and clear,
Making us a country dear.
That is why we all are here."

Poetry writing was hard work, Mollie decided. Perhaps she really was no good. Her brain was beginning to ache, and she was getting silly. "Easter bunny, Easter egg, standing on a chicken leg . . ."

She stretched, she yawned. She looked out of the bedroom window. The afternoon sun was still bright. On the sidewalk Shelley was roller skating alone up and down between her house and Mollie's.

"Hey, Shell," Mollie yelled out the window. "Wait a minute. I'll be right down."

She got her roller skates from the hall closet and went outside.

"I thought you had something important to do," Shelley said.

"It wasn't as important as I thought."

"Want some cake or a banana?"

"No, thanks." Mollie bent over to tighten her skates.

The two girls skated silently for a while from one end of the block to the other. Once, when they passed Shelley's house, the smell of baking came through the door.

"Your mother's always making something," Mollie said.

"Yeah."

"How come she doesn't go to work?"

"Why should she?"

"I dunno." Apparently, the Depression hadn't come as far as Shelley's house, Mollie thought.

They sat on Shelley's front steps and removed their skates. Mollie swung hers back and forth from the straps. They were heavy.

"My father says that your mother has to work because your father has no more clients," Shelley said, as if she had been thinking about it for some time.

Mollie looked up angrily and a little surprised. It was not like Shelley to say something mean. "My father has clients, plenty of them. They just don't pay him."

"If you ever want anything to eat . . ." Shelley began kindly.

"You think we're poor?" Mollie shouted. "You think my father doesn't bring home any money?" Shelley backed away. "We have plenty of money. My mother works because she wants to help the sick people. She really doesn't have to, you know. If she wanted to, she could stay home all day and cook and bake and lie around listening to the radio and getting fat like your mother. She just doesn't want to." Mollie's arm holding the skates went up over her head. She was about to send them crashing down on Shelley's skull, she was so angry.

She flicked them like a whip for more power, but instead of crushing Shelley's head, the weight of the skates slammed into Mollie's back. She fell to the ground, furious and aching.

35

"Are you all right?" Shelley asked, bending over her.
Mollie, dazed for the moment, lay there. She could feel her skinned knees and her aching shoulders. She raised her head to look at Shelley.

"I might have really hurt you," she said, bewildered. "Except that the skates were so heavy . . ."

She stood up slowly and brushed at her bleeding knees. "Do you believe in God?" she asked.

Shelley's mouth hung open.

In Mollie's mind there could be no other explanation. The hand of God, not the skates, really, had knocked her over. The idea had come to her as she lay on the ground. He had saved Shelley from a broken head and her from becoming a murderer! She gave Shelley a long, slow look and turned around toward her own house.

"I'll call for you tomorrow," Shelley said. "O.K.?"

"O.K.," Mollie answered, swinging her skates slowly back and forth as she walked away.

CHAPTER *Six*

"I was almost a murderer," Mollie kept thinking. "I almost killed Shelley."

She had seen murderers on The March of Time—real ones, that is, not like Humphrey Bogart or James Cagney, who were really actors playing murderers. There was one, a kidnapper who had taken a little baby from his crib. But she had never seen an eleven-year-old girl murderer— not even in a movie. Jane Withers was mean to Shirley Temple, but she never killed anyone.

There she would be on the movie screen, handcuffed and being dragged down the hall to the electric chair.

"I don't want to die. I'm too young to die," she would scream just like Edward G. Robinson or those others. And her friends would sit there, waiting for Flash Gordon to come on, snapping their bubble gum and crackling candy wrappers and not paying any attention.

Except, probably, Florette and Elaine. They always told about the famous people they or their parents knew.

"You know Cary Grant? Well, my mother met a lady who has his autograph." Or, "My cousin used to live next door to the cousin of a man who works for the Major Bowes Amateur Hour."

Of course, she would never tell them what almost happened, but she could picture them saying, "You know the girl who hit Shelley with her skates? We live on the same block, and she bought her skates at Higgins' Toy Shop, the same place we bought ours."

But now they couldn't say that, and Mollie could not stop wondering why.

"If someone was going to do something bad to someone else and all of a sudden something stopped him, what do you think?" Mollie asked her mother as she swept the kitchen floor after dinner.

"Can you be a little more specific?" her mother said impatiently. "There are an awful lot of someones and somethings in that question."

Mollie thought for a minute. She didn't want to tell exactly what she meant. "I mean, say, if a person got really angry at another person and took a . . . a . . . knife to kill that other person and then the knife . . . the knife turned into a banana, what would that be?"

"A miracle," her father interrupted, "it would be a miracle, and a rather delicious one at that. Do we have any bananas, Edith?"

"Too expensive this week," Mrs. Stone said. "Have an apple."

She pointed to the icebox. "A man was selling them outside the hospital entrance, and he looked so miserable that I bought two. I kept thinking, 'There but for the grace of God go you.'"

Mollie's father smiled. "It's not that bad, Edith. At least, not so far. I'm not selling apples on a corner yet."

Mollie put the broom away and went to the window. She could see the light go out in the kitchen of Shelley's house. "Grace of God, there but for the grace of God I could be in prison," she said to herself.

It seemed like the right answer.

Two steps at a time, which was not ladylike, her mother always told her, Mollie raced up the stairs to her bedroom. She took a fresh piece of paper from her notebook and

39

brushed the rest of her schoolbooks off the little desk. Then she began a search for a pencil without a broken point.

"Ah ha!" she said, discovering one hidden beneath her speller.

She sat down at the desk, curled her legs around the front legs of the chair so that her toes pointed in opposite directions, and began.

The words came rushing out so fast that Mollie could barely put them on the paper. It had taken her no longer than ten minutes it seemed, and she was sure it would win the contest. Almost in amazement, she read her words.

> "Who pulls the sun from behind the hill
> To make it morning bright
> And takes away the damp and chill
> That comes with the black of night?
>
> "Who paints the sky such a brilliant hue
> And then lets it fade into gray?
> It is not you or you or you
> Who makes it the end of day.
>
> "Who lights the moon and the stars above
> That into my bedroom shine?
> It's God, you say? Then it's He I love.
> God, please be my Valentine."

Mollie carefully read the contest rules that Miss Felt had written on the blackboard.
1. Neatly written—penmanship counts.
2. Margins exactly one inch on both sides of the paper.
3. Name, school, class in upper left-hand corner.
4. Title two lines above first stanza.
5. Do not write on both sides of the paper.
6. No erasures or crossing out!
7. Ink—not pencil!

Mollie took another clean sheet of notebook paper and followed the instructions.

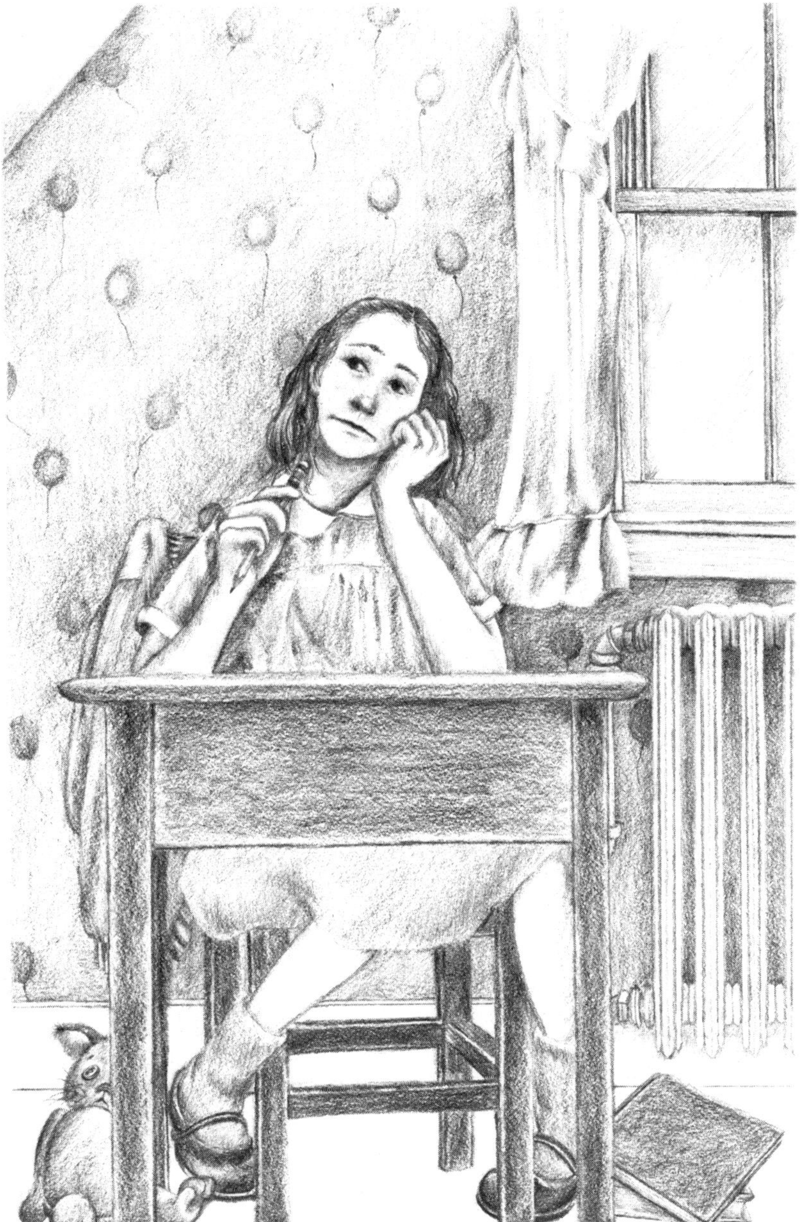

When she had finished, she stared at the sheet of writing trying to see it as the judges might. She pictured them discussing it among themselves. "Marvelous poem!" "A great talent!" they would say as they lean over the table on which her poem lies. It shines in the sunlight, and the judges wipe tears from their eyes and blow their noses loudly as they behold its beauty.

She could see herself walking up the steps of the auditorium stage in cousin Rhoda's blue dress that her mother had shortened. Her black patent leather Mary Jane shoes make a squeaky sound as the leather heels tap across the stage.

"Mollie Stone, how can we tell you what a wonderful poem you wrote? The only way is to present you with this check for ten dollars and the gratefulness of the world." And Mr. Guss would shake her hand and so would Miss Conklin.

She couldn't wait to hand it in on Monday morning.

CHAPTER *Seven*

At school, Mollie sat behind Mignon Swenson, who was so fat that Mollie had to lean halfway into the aisle to see the blackboard. When Miss Felt was being very boring, as she always was in arithmetic, Mollie would study the part down the middle of Mignon's head and the two braided circles of hair that wound around each side of her head like earmuffs and then Mignon's fat neck disappearing into the embroidered peasant blouses she always wore.

Everyone knew that Mignon was very smart. She played the piano sometimes at assemblies and always knew the answers when Miss Felt called on her.

Mollie neither liked nor disliked her. As a matter of fact, she hardly knew her, although they had been in the same classes since third grade when Mignon moved to town. She always went home for lunch in a big black car that her mother drove and never lingered after school to play in the schoolyard.

Mollie had no idea at all where Mignon lived and so was very surprised, one day, to find an invitation from her tucked into one of her books. It was an invitation to lunch on the following Saturday written neatly and signed not by Mignon, but by her mother, Mrs. Swenson, Henrietta Swenson to be exact.

Mollie slipped it to Shelley while Miss Felt was unrolling a large map of the United States over the blackboard. Shelley bent her head to read it under her desk, then raised her eyebrows in question.

Mollie raised hers back and shrugged her shoulders, but this method of communication was unsatisfactory, so Mollie wrote a note. "Are you invited, too? How come she didn't ask me in person? Did you ever hear of anything so kookoo? Ha ha."

". . . the Louisiana Purchase in what year, Mollie?"

At the sound of her name, Mollie jumped. Miss Felt was staring at her. "What?" Mollie asked.

"You seem to be so busy writing, I thought you might have some important thoughts for us to share."

"What?" Mollie repeated.

"May I see what you are passing around the room?" Miss Felt held out her hand to Shelley.

"I was just telling . . ." Mollie began, but Shelley, always obedient, had marched up to Miss Felt and handed her the invitation.

Miss Felt read it slowly, looked at Mignon, then at Mollie and back again at Mignon, whose face and neck were changing from white to deep red. Miss Felt smiled at her. "Isn't that nice?" was all she said, and handed the invitation back to Mollie. "Now, who can tell me the year of the Louisiana Purchase?"

It had happened again, Mollie noticed, some sort of magic touch that Mignon had. She never got into trouble, and now she appeared able to save anyone connected with her from getting into trouble. Mollie felt sure it had something to do with her mother being president of the PTA, although she was not sure why this was so. As far as she knew, all the PTA did was hand out shriveled apples to each student on the day before Christmas vacation.

At dinner that night, she showed her mother the invitation.

"Who is Mrs. Swenson?" her mother asked.

"She's the mother of Mignon, a girl in my class."

"I've never heard you mention Mignon. Is she someone new?"

"She's been in my class since third grade."

"Is this a birthday party?" Mrs. Stone asked, as confused as Mollie about the invitation. After all, with the exception of birthday parties, written invitations came only for weddings or, in the days before the Depression, from clients and friends whose houses you had to take a train or drive to. Mollie had been invited many times for lunch by Shelley or Florette while playing at their houses, but never by written invitation.

"No, I don't think so. At least it doesn't say, does it?" She examined the note again in case she had missed something.

"No, it doesn't," her mother agreed. "Well, if you want to go . . ."

"I don't know. I mean, I hardly know her. I mean, why should she invite me when she never even talks to me in school?"

"Maybe she's lonely," her father said. "Perhaps she's too shy to approach you."

Mollie laughed. "Shy? She's as big as a horse."

"I don't see the connection," Mr. Stone said.

"Probably a glandular condition," Mrs. Stone said.

"Do glands make you shy?" Danny asked. "I must have real good glands. I'm not shy at all."

Everyone seemed to have forgotten about the invitation, and because the conversation interested Mollie, she didn't mention it again. Mollie liked hearing her mother talk about medical things—like glands. Her mother seldom did, although she felt Mollie's and Danny's pulses when they were sick. Her mother's world during the day was a mystery, and Mollie often pictured her walking through hospital wards full of groaning soldiers—wearing a long gray skirt and carrying a lamp like the picture of Florence Nightingale in her history book.

"How was the hospital today?" Mollie asked, hoping her mother would tell her everything that happened.

"Busy."

"Did anyone die or have some dreadful disease?"

"Quite a few."

"I know. I mean, what kind of diseases?"

"Oh, some of them have broken bones, some have malnutrition, some . . . Danny, you're spilling your milk!"

And that ended the conversation.

For the next few days, Mollie tried to catch Mignon's eye, seeking some hint that she wanted to be friendly. Several times she approached her asking about homework assignments, but Mignon answered only what was necessary—"Page 43 in the arithmetic book," or, "Study the names of the thirteen colonies for Wednesday."

On Friday, however, she walked over to Mollie during the assembly lineup. "See you tomorrow," she whispered like a secret spy, "17 Blake Street."

On Saturday morning, Mollie awoke with the feeling that something was supposed to happen that day. She remembered Mignon. Actually, she had never told Mignon that she was coming, but it seemed that Mignon never doubted it.

She dressed, wondering whether she would have to change for lunch. Her old green jumper seemed good enough, and she rubbed her scuffed brown shoes with the edge of the bedspread until they shone.

Three hours to wait until twelve-thirty, the hour the invitation had mentioned. She made her bed, swept the kitchen floor, offered to do the ironing for her mother but was refused, as usual, because she did not know how and her mother, as usual, was too rushed to teach her. She followed her father around as he weeded the tiny flower beds along the walk and eventually went over to Shelley's house, where she found Mr. Weller lying on the sofa reading the paper.

"Went shopping with my wife," Shelley's father said. "Back after lunch."

Mollie watched his big, black moustache bobbing up and down as he spoke. When she was younger, she used to think that he had swallowed a cat with two tails. Even though he was a nice man, she was still a little afraid of him.

"I'll come back later," she called from the doorway.

"Yes, later," Mr. Weller answered.

She returned home, brushed her hair, and straightened the barrette that held the clump at the top of her head.

"I'm going," she said to her mother, who was finishing the last of her father's shirt.

"Where, may I ask?"

"To Mignon's for lunch."

"Wait a minute. Carry these things upstairs, please."

"I'll do it when I come home. O.K.?"

"I can imagine," her mother said, piling her own arms full of freshly ironed clothes.

Mollie kissed her quickly.

"Have a good time," her mother called, "and don't eat like a pig."

CHAPTER *Eight*

Mignon's house was on the other side of Charlotte Avenue, where the houses were separated from each other by clumps of trees and wide lawns. It was white with green shutters, and the door was opened by a skinny woman wearing a white uniform and bedroom slippers.

Mollie thought at first she was a nurse and that Mignon was sick and no one had remembered to tell her not to come. But the woman motioned for her to come in. From another room, the sound of a piano could be heard.

"Is this where Mignon lives?" Mollie asked the woman.

"Yeah, are you the one come for lunch?"

"Yes, Mignon gave me this invitation . . ."

The woman, still facing Mollie, raised her head and called loudly, "Someone is here to see you, Minnie."

As if it were some sort of signal, Mignon's mother appeared at the top of the stairs. She was wearing a long black dress and a hat with flowers on it. "Della, how many times have I told you not to call my daughter Minnie?"

" 'Bout four thousand nine hundred and seventy-eight," Della said with a wink at Mollie. Mollie, startled at this suddenly friendly expression, smiled back weakly.

Mrs. Swenson came down the stairs slowly, one hand on the railing. "You must be Mollie." She didn't smile when she spoke, just stared into Mollie's face.

"Yes, I am." Mollie stared back and realized that Mrs.

48

Swenson was not wearing a hat at all but a lot of hair piled high on her head with a big rose stuck into the top layer. She was very tall and skinny. Mollie thought, "This is how Mignon would look if she were rolled out."

Mrs. Swenson took her by the shoulder and turned her toward a large room off the hall. "Mignon, your guest is here."

Mignon slid toward the edge of the piano bench but did not get up. She looked at a spot somewhere far above Mollie's head. "Hello," she mumbled.

"Hi," Mollie said.

"Luncheon will be ready in a few minutes. Why don't you two girls just sit and chat for a moment? I'll see how Della's doing."

"I didn't know you lived here," Mollie said after Mrs. Swenson had left.

"Yes, this is where I live."

"Your mother said I could sit."

"O.K., sit."

Mollie sat down in the nearest chair. It was much too deep, and her legs stuck out in front of her like a rag doll's. She studied her shoes, noticed she had missed polishing a spot, and moved to the edge of the chair to rub the dirty shoe against the back of her leg.

Mignon watched her silently.

"An itch," Mollie explained.

Mignon shook her head as if Mollie had just told her something very important. Mollie then scratched her arm, her nose, and her thigh to make sure Mignon believed her.

"Do you have a rash?" Mignon asked.

"Huh?"

"You keep scratching yourself," Mignon said.

Mollie coughed loudly. "Hey, Mignon, how come you invited me here?" she asked.

Mignon did not seem upset by the question. "My mother made me."

"Yeah? How come?"

49

"I think she wants to pickle your brain," Mignon said with a little laugh.

Before Mollie could say anything, Mrs. Swenson stuck her head in the door. "Luncheon is served," she called.

Three places were set in the dining room, which was quite dark, lit only by two tall candles in the center of the table.

"Mollie, you sit over there." Mrs. Swenson pointed to one of the places.

Mignon took the seat across from Mollie, and Mollie, not wishing to look at her, glanced around the room. On the wall behind Mignon, an enormous ugly face stuck out of the wall. Mollie stared at it, wondering if it were a picture of one of Mignon's relatives. Then, as her eyes became used to the half darkness, she saw that it was a giant mask, with white paint around the eyes and mouth and a big gold ring hanging from the nose. Tufts of hair rose from the top of the mask, also painted white.

"Someone with pickled brains," Mollie thought, a little frightened.

"Oh, you noticed the African mask," Mrs. Swenson said. "Mr. Swenson brought it back from one of his trips abroad. Now then, Mollie, how are you enjoying school?"

"It's O.K."

"Mignon finds her history assignments very stimulating, don't you, Mignon?"

"They're O.K.," Mignon said in exactly the same voice as Mollie's.

"What business is your father in, Mollie?"

"He's a lawyer." Mollie looked at the bowl of soup Della had placed in front of her. It was green and had things floating around in it.

"Isn't that nice, a lawyer. I knew you would be a nice friend for Mignon. Help yourself to a roll, Mollie."

Mollie reached for a large roll, but for some reason her hand picked up the smallest on the dish.

"And your mother? I don't believe I've seen her at the PTA meetings."

"Ah ha," Mollie thought. "So that's why I was invited. Mrs. Swenson wants my mother to join the PTA."

"Well, she's very busy during the day, but she told me she wanted to come sometime." The last part was certainly not true; Mollie's mother thought the PTA was full of "idle women who have nothing better to do than to go to the beauty parlor and admire each other's hats."

"What keeps her so busy? I suppose you have a large family to care for?"

"No, just me and my brother and my father."

"Well, then what keeps her so busy? Does she work?"

Della, standing behind Mignon's chair with a tray of celery and tomatoes, looked at Mrs. Swenson angrily. Mollie thought she was about to say something, but instead she just kept staring at her employer.

"She's a nurse, but not for money. She has to take care of my brother," Mollie blurted out. "He has a glandular condition."

Mignon looked up from her plate and stared at Mollie. "I thought your brother was in the second grade at school."

"Oh, that's my other brother, my little one. My big brother never leaves his room. That's why I forget about him sometimes. He has to lie in bed all day, and my mother gives him expensive medicine and takes his temperature and feels his pulse every twenty minutes in case he should die." Mollie took a big bite of the roll.

"How awful!" Mrs. Swenson gasped. "The poor dear, your poor mother!"

"I hope you're satisfied," Della said loudly, but Mrs. Swenson just kept staring at Mollie.

Mollie toyed with the chocolate cake that Della had placed in front of her. She wondered if Mrs. Swenson really was pickling her brain because ever since she had entered this house, she had done nothing but tell lies—starting with the little one about her itch and building up to this big one about a sick brother that she didn't have.

"I have to go now," Mollie said suddenly. "I have to—I have to care for my brother while my mother takes a rest." She stood up.

"Oh, dear, I am so sorry," Mrs. Swenson said. "I had hoped that you and Mignon would play together. Of all the children in her class, you seemed to have most in common with Mignon, especially the fact that you're both poets."

Mollie froze for a moment. Then she turned around slowly. "How do you know?"

"Why Miss Felt told me you are one of the children who submitted a little poem. I think that's lovely. Now why don't you stay? Mignon is so fond of you."

"Oh, Mother, what did you have to say that for?" Mignon threw down her napkin and began to cry.

"I've got to go. My brother may be dying this very moment," Mollie shouted over her shoulder.

"Come again," Mrs. Swenson called.

"Don't count on it," Della said loudly.

Mollie ran all the way home, the full eight blocks, and was breathless as she entered.

"Good grief, what happened to you?" her father asked as he opened the door. "How was that lunch with the written invitation?"

"Pretty good. I mean it tasted all right, but I couldn't see what it was."

"Over so fast? You've only been gone an hour," her mother asked.

"I came home to help you, er, carry up the laundry."

"How thoughtful," her father said.

"Too late," her mother said.

"Another lie," Mollie thought.

CHAPTER *Nine*

Mollie was convinced that Mignon and her mother had cast some sort of spell over her. How else could anyone explain the lies she had told?

She felt a funny, uncomfortable feeling in her stomach every time she thought about the luncheon and was annoyed when Shelley asked her about it on the way to school Monday.

"It was O.K."

"Did you see Mignon's room?" Shelley was always anxious to know about other people's houses, especially other girls' bedrooms. Hers was full of flowers—on the wallpaper, on the curtains, on the bedspreads, and even painted on her dresser. She thought it was beautiful, but it made Mollie feel she was suffocating whenever she visited.

"I didn't stay too long."

"Why did she invite you in the first place?"

"I guess her mother wanted me to be her friend."

"Does she have lots of dolls? Does she have a swing? I heard she had a swing."

"I didn't see it."

"What did you have to eat? Something good?"

"Oh, some soup and . . . I forget."

"Was anyone else there?"

"Me, her mother, Mignon, and the maid."

"The maid! Mignon has a maid?"

This bit of information was worth all the other answers put together.

"Her name is Della."

"Did she wear a uniform? Did she . . . ?"

"Shelley, quit asking all those questions! I just don't feel like talking about it."

"Why? Were they mean to you?"

Mollie wanted to say something to shut Shelley up, and the thought that had been in her mind for the whole weekend came bursting out. "I think they're both witches!"

Shelley laughed. "What are you talking about?"

"Well"—Mollie thought fast—"don't you think it's kind of strange that Mignon never gets into trouble and that all the teachers smile and practically bow down when Mrs. Swenson comes into the school and that Mignon never gets anything but A's on her tests and . . . ?" She had run out of reasons except for the one that she didn't want to discuss.

"Well, she *is* president of the PTA, and Mignon always does her homework," Shelley said.

"Just think about it, Shell, just think about it," Mollie said.

It was clear to Shelley that Mollie had some information that she was not telling, some real proof that lay hidden somewhere in Mignon's house. After all, Mollie had been there and no one else had. She could not picture Mrs. Swenson in one of those pointed hats that everyone wore in the Halloween play, but maybe Mollie had seen one in the back of a closet somewhere. "A witch?" Shelley asked.

"Oh, forget it."

By noon, the whole class was whispering and pointing

to Mignon. Shelley was not one to keep such fascinating information to herself.

"Did she try to cast a spell on you?" Florette whispered to Mollie.

"Who?" Mollie's heart gave a little flip.

"You know." Florette pointed to Mignon.

Mollie just shrugged her shoulders.

Florette looked knowingly at Elaine, who passed the look on to Herbert. It went up and down the rows of seats, skipping Mignon, whose fat shoulders were hunched over a history book, and finally was picked up by Miss Felt.

"May I ask what is going on here?" She was truly curious; there was no actual disturbance in the class, just a feeling that something was causing a good deal of distraction. Miss Felt was not even sure whom she should ask.

The class sat innocently, hands folded, all staring back at the teacher.

"Now, just behave yourselves." The atmosphere of the room was heavy with stifled giggles, but no one made a sound.

Suddenly, Mignon raised her hand. "Miss Felt, may I leave the room?"

Miss Felt smiled. "Certainly, Mignon. Why, Mignon, is something the matter?"

The children in the back leaned as far forward as they could; those in the front turned around. Mignon's face was puffier than usual and her eyes were very red. With a great sob, she rushed from the room, Miss Felt chasing after her.

Immediately, everyone began to talk at once. There was no one to stop them. They crowded around Mollie asking questions, commenting on Mignon's strange behavior, all declaring they could not imagine what was wrong. "I didn't say anything," Florette said. "Me neither," everyone else agreed.

Mollie, uncomfortable at being the center of attraction

and feeling a little guilty that she might be the cause of Mignon's tears, kept repeating, "Get away, get away. Leave me alone."

The school secretary had come in, causing everyone to slide back into his seat. "Which is Mignon's desk?" she asked. They pointed to it. "And did she have a coat or anything?" No one knew.

"Is Mignon sick?" someone asked innocently.

"Just give me her books," the secretary said, and thirty hands rushed to be of assistance. "Miss Felt will be coming back, so just be quiet." She left the room, passing Miss Felt in the doorway.

"Is Mignon sick?" Florette asked.

Miss Felt narrowed her eyes at the class.

Mollie waited for her name to be spoken, for a message from Miss Conklin's office, for some mighty blow to fall on her head. She sat frozen in her seat. If Mrs. Swenson really was a witch, she could reach out and change the entire class into toads or make them disappear into thin air, never to be seen again. She wondered if their clothes would disappear, too, or if little piles of dresses and pants and shirts would be left behind, empty and folded on the classroom floor.

Nothing happened. Miss Felt said, "Yes, Mignon is not feeling well, and let's get on with our arithmetic. We've wasted enough time."

Mrs. Swenson was not a witch.

CHAPTER *Ten*

"Just like they were movie stars," Shelley was complaining. "Why, do you know that Elaine said she might wear lipstick to school? And silk stockings? Just because that Uncle Pat said they would be on the radio show. Boy, I mean how stuck up can you get?"

Mollie was not listening. She was busy reading the envelopes that had come in the mail. Both girls were in Mollie's living room, Mollie on the sofa with the pile of letters in her lap, her school books thrown down beside her. Shelley was at the piano bench, tickling the keys so that each time she spoke her words were accompanied by some strange music.

"Hey, here's a letter from Boston," Mollie said, holding the envelope up to the light.

"I think I'm going to throw up if they mention the show once more," Shelley said with a bang on the piano.

"It's probably from my Aunt Ruth."

"And another thing, did you see how Elaine's hair was piled on her head?" Shelley giggled. "My mother said she looked like a washerwoman."

"My Aunt Ruth lives in Boston. I visit her sometimes. Once I took the train all by myself and stayed two weeks over Christmas."

"I never go anywhere," Shelley said. "Except once.

58

Once I went to the mountains. I was so little, though, I don't remember it. They had a lake and a big dining room. I guess it was a hotel. I wish I could remember it."

"Hey, look, Shell, recognize this handwriting?" Mollie threw one of the other envelopes to Shelley. It landed on the floor, and Shelley, too lazy to bend over, tried to read it from where she sat.

"Let's see." She squinted and twisted her head. "Who's it addressed to, you?"

With a sigh, Mollie got up, picked up the envelope, and pushed it under Shelley's nose. "Boy, are you blind! It's to my mother. Don't you recognize the handwriting?"

"You're holding it too close. Let's see. Where does it come from? I mean what's the postmark?"

"You are really dumb!" Mollie said, pulling the letter away. "It's from Mrs. Swenson. It's the same writing as on the invitation."

Shelley jumped up. "Don't touch it!" she screamed. "It could be poisoned. It could have a spell on it!"

Mollie thought about it for a moment and put the letter on the piano. She was sure there was no spell on it, but it probably meant trouble in another way. She wondered if she should just by accident slide it under the rug or in the piano bench between her music books.

"Wanta do something?" Shelley asked. "Wanta come over to my house and have something to eat? Or roller skate? Or jump rope?"

Mollie weighed the letters in one hand. She slid the one from Mrs. Swenson to the bottom of the pile and placed them on the kitchen table.

"Maybe my Aunt Ruth wants me to come for vacation. Gee, maybe I'll be spending the summer in Boston with my cousins." She thought about the possibility. She had a great time with her cousins Bobby, Jon, and Gordon. Of course, she hardly saw Gordon; he was seventeen and did not bother too much with eleven-year-old girl cousins. But

Bobby and Jon were just a little older than Mollie, and they took her to the movies and to their friends' houses and on ice skating jaunts. "Boy, I hope Aunt Ruth wants me to come." Mollie sighed.

Shelley looked unhappy. "You mean you'd be gone for the whole summer? That's a long time. I mean, who would I play with?"

"Oh, you could play with Florette and Elaine," Mollie said lightly.

"Them? Are you kidding? Why I wouldn't play with them if they . . ."

"Ooh hoo," someone outside was calling. "Ooh hoo, anybody home?"

"Who goes there?" Mollie called. "Friend or foe, someone I know or just Joe Blow?"

A high giggle sounded, and Elaine's head, with its brown curls bouncing, appeared at the window.

"Whatcha want?" Mollie said, trying to sound like a movie tough guy.

"Florette is inviting you to come over to her house. We have something to tell you. We have a surprise. C'mon over."

"Shelley's here," Mollie called.

"Bring her along. Hi, Shell."

"She won't come. She said she wouldn't play . . ."

Shelley came bounding across the room. "Mollie, don't tell them that." Then she turned to the window. "Hello, Elaine." Then back to Mollie, "Let's go?" she said as if it were a question.

"What's the surprise?" Mollie asked through the window.

"It wouldn't be a surprise if I told you, would it?"

"It's not one of your rehearsals, is it?"

"Listen, are you coming or not?" Elaine's head was drawing back from the window.

"Well, I was going to practice the piano," Mollie lied. "And then I have this important engagement."

Shelley pulled her by the arm. "Let's go."

The three girls walked slowly across the street and up to Florette's house and through the house to the back porch.

The surprise was, Mollie noted with a lurch of her heart, that Mignon was sitting on Florette's back porch looking very white in the late afternoon sunlight and very silent.

"Hi, Florette, hi, Mignon," Shelley said.

"Hey, how come . . . ?" Mollie started to say. Florette and Elaine didn't know Mignon any better than she did —as a matter of fact, not even as well.

Elaine's fingers grabbed Mollie by the arm and dragged her into a corner. "We felt sorry for her," she whispered, "and we need a person to play the piano. Anyhow, her father gave my father a ride to the bus stop the other day. Her father has a big car, my father says."

Mollie looked at Mignon from the corner of her eye. "I saw her car, and it's not that big," she whispered back to Elaine.

Elaine was not sure whether to laugh or not. She tossed her head so that the Tootsie Roll curls hit Mollie in the eye.

"Hey!" Mollie yelled.

Mignon snickered.

Florette was busy writing at the bridge table that took up most of the tiny porch. She glanced up and nodded her head. Mignon stretched her lips in a make-believe smile and then let them bounce back as if they were made of rubber. The make-believe smile was directed only at Shelley.

Mollie sat down on a small wooden rocking chair near the back door. Slowly she rocked back and forth. "So here we are from near and far, har, har, har."

"Oh, yes, Mollie the poet," Mignon said. "What a beautiful poem!"

"Well, it was not one of my best, but what can one do on such short notice?" Mollie replied in an imitation of Miss Felt's English accent.

Florette put down the pencil. "O.K., we're all set."

"Set for what?" Shelley asked.

"For our show," Florette said.

"Hey, wait a minute," Mollie said, rocking faster and faster. "I thought you said this wasn't going to be a rehearsal. C'mon, Shell—let's go back."

"It's not a rehearsal. It's a kind of . . . well, you're going to be in it and Mignon and . . . and . . . Shelley. Shelley, do you do anything?"

"What do you mean, do I do anything? Like what?"

"Oh," Elaine explained, "like singing, dancing, playing the piano." She smiled at Mignon.

Before Shelley could answer, Mollie jumped up from her rocker. "As you know, my dear Songbirds, I don't do anything either."

"Oh, yes you do," Mignon said slyly. "You're a poet. You could recite a tragic poem about your dear dying brother and how hard your mother works and we would all cry."

Elaine had already begun. A large tear squeezed out of her eye. "You're brother is dying? Oh, how terrible!"

Mignon grunted like a pig. "Not her little brother. Her big big brother. Isn't that right, Mollie?"

"But," Shelley said, "Mollie doesn't have a big brother. At least I don't think she does. At least, I never knew she did. Do you, Mollie?"

"Oh, Mignon's just trying to start trouble. She's never even been in my house."

"I don't have to go to your house," Mignon said, sticking out her tongue. "My mother looked up the records at school and found out. Nyah."

"Hey," Shelley said brightly. "Maybe that's what her letter was about, huh, Mollie?"

"Oh, shut up," Mollie said, sitting down heavily in the rocker.

"I declare," Elaine remarked in a sudden southern accent. "I don't know whatever you folks are talking about. Let's get back to the show, anyway."

Florette cleared her throat. "Now, we thought it would be a good idea to have a show, something like Uncle Pat's on the radio. Just sort of to get us used to performing with other people." She said the last words quickly before Mollie could protest that it was a rehearsal they were planning. "Now"—she consulted her list—"Elaine and I will do our duet, Mignon will play the piano, Mollie will recite one of her poems, and Shelley . . . can you tap-dance, Shell?"

Shelley thought carefully. "No, but I can put some toilet paper over a comb and go Mmmm."

Florette rolled her eyes to the heavens. "Maybe Shelley can be the announcer."

"Sure," Shelley said. "Listen, I talk very well. Ladies and gentlemen, welcome to . . . to . . . the show."

"Wonderful," Mollie said, "you talk very nicely. You must have been doing that all your life."

"Not until I was a year and a half . . ." Shelley started.

"Oh, shut up," Mollie mumbled.

"Well, Herbert was going to announce, but now I guess he'll tell one of his jokes," Florette said, crossing something off her list.

"Do you have a poem for me to recite, or can I pick one of my own?" Mollie asked as if she weren't the slightest bit interested in the answer.

"Mignon says you're so good at making them up. Can't you do that?"

"Listen, Mignon, how do you know how good I am? Did you ever see a poem I wrote?" Mollie asked angrily.

"No, and I doubt anyone else did either," Mignon answered.

"What does that mean?" Mollie asked. Actually, she thought that by now Mrs. Swenson would have read her contest poem.

63

"Forget it," Mignon said.

"When is this show going to be?" Shelley asked.

"Saturday morning, just like Uncle Pat's. Only ours will be right after so we can hear him," Florette said.

"Who's going to see this wonderful show?" Mollie asked. "Are you going to charge admission or something?"

"No, of course not. We'll just invite . . . well, whoever wants to come."

A voice came from somewhere not too far away. "Shelleeee, Shelleeee, cuuuum hooome for suuupper."

"Your mother's calling you," Florette said. "After school tomorrow I'll write down what you're supposed to say. We'll all meet here again."

"Same time, same station," Elaine said.

Shelley walked through the house to the front door.

"Wait, I'm coming with you," Mollie said, racing after her.

"Tomorrow," Florette called. "Don't forget—and bring a poem."

"Yeah, sure," Mollie mumbled. "Hey, Shelley, do you want to be in their dumb show?"

"Sure," Shelley said, shaking her head. "Don't you?"

"Yeah, how's this for a poem? Mignon, Florette, Elaine sure give me a pain."

Shelley giggled, waved, and ran into her house. Mollie continued the few steps to her own house, where she found her mother at the kitchen table reading the mail.

CHAPTER *Eleven*

"Dear Edith," Mollie read over her mother's shoulder. "I hope everything is well with you and the children and Ben. I suppose you are wondering why I'm writing to you. Well, I don't know how to begin, but I guess I'll have to.

"Things have not been going too well here. Arthur has had to take a cut in salary for the next term. I'm sure you know that teachers don't make much anyway, but we thank God that he has a job. It's more than some men have these horrible days. Of course, it means that Gordon won't be able to go to college in the fall. I don't know what he will do—but, this is not what I'm writing to you about. Edith, do you remember my neighbors the Altmans, who came here from Poland a few years ago? They came to dinner once when you visited—with their children, two girls Anna and Frances, very nice children. Well, poor Mr. Altman killed himself—turned on the gas when nobody was home—after he lost his job in the factory. And his wife is now in a hospital completely out of her mind. I tell you it has been just terrible for those two girls. They have nobody, no relatives in America, nobody!

"I have had them both living with me, but it has been very hard. Now, with Arthur making less money, it will be impossible to keep them both. Edith, I know what a good woman you are and Ben, how kind he is. And I know, too, that things have not been going well for you either what with Ben's clients not paying him. But think how it would be if Mollie and Danny were left alone—with nobody—and I know that you will take one of the girls to live with you until things get better. Frances can take care of the house and stay with the children and make life easier for you in many ways. She doesn't eat much and has enough clothes to last for a while. She is very quiet and will not bother anyone. I am keeping Anna, the younger one, because she is still in school and wants to finish here in Boston.

"God will bless you, Edith, I am sure for doing this."

Aunt Ruth then wrote how and when Frances was coming.

"She doesn't eat much, your Aunt Ruth says." Mollie's mother shook her head in disagreement. "Even a bird would be an extra burden these days with steak twenty-five cents a pound and milk ten cents a quart."

"A bird burden—that's funny, Mom," Mollie said, trying to make her mother laugh.

Mrs. Stone didn't laugh, but she smiled at her daughter.

"Well, what can we do? I suppose we will have to take Frances in. We'll manage somehow. Those poor little things have had to go through so much." She looked as if she were about to cry, and Mollie asked very quickly, "When is she coming?"

For the third time, Mrs. Stone examined the letter. "Saturday morning. She'll be here Saturday morning. That's very soon, isn't it?"

Mollie shook her head yes.

"We'll have to make her feel welcome, Mollie," Mrs. Stone said, and to Mollie's great surprise she grabbed her and hugged her hard, kissing the top of Mollie's head. "This shows you how lucky we are. At least we have each other."

"M-m-m," Mollie mumbled to the button on her mother's blouse that was pressing against her nose. She was almost in tears, too, but just in time her mother let go.

"Now," she said, sniffing the way Mollie often did when she was too lazy to find a handkerchief, "call your brother, please."

Mollie went out to the back porch, cupped her hands around her mouth, and shouted, "Danny, come home. Danny, come home."

In a few seconds Danny appeared behind the cherry tree. "Here I am. What do you want?"

"Nothin'. Mom just said to call you." Mollie, having completed that task, went in to set the table.

"You know, Mom, next week at this time you won't have to cook and I won't have to set the table. We'll have a maid, just like the Swensons."

Mrs. Stone whirled around, her eyes still sparkling but her face angry. "Don't you ever say that again! Frances will not be our servant. She'll be a member of the family, a sort of cousin. Is that clear, young lady?"

"I guess so." Mollie wondered how her mother's feelings could change so fast. "Anyhow, what's so bad about being a servant? It's a job, isn't it?"

Mrs. Stone looked at her daughter for a moment with a little half-smile on her lips. "It's not the job I'm thinking about. It's some people's attitude about work around here."

Mollie, to change the subject, asked, "Is that all the mail there is? I thought I saw some other letters."

"Oh, nothing important," Mrs. Stone said, stirring something in a pot. "Just a note from Mrs. Swenson saying that she hoped Danny was feeling better. She must have me mixed up with someone else."

CHAPTER *Twelve*

For the first time since she had been in school, Mollie was called out of class to Miss Conklin's office. The school secretary had come in and whispered something to Miss Felt, who nodded a "Behave yourselves" nod to the class and left. After the secretary had slid into Miss Felt's chair, she pointed to Mollie, then turned the same finger around and wiggled it. Mollie came up to the desk.

"Miss Conklin wants to see you," she said softly.

"Why?" Mollie asked, but she knew that the secretary would not explain. She would only smile.

As she walked down the hall, Mollie tried to think about what she had done to be called down to the principal. Nothing came into her mind except the loud thump, thump of her heart, which she was sure everyone behind the closed classroom doors could hear.

When she arrived, the principal, Miss Felt, and Mrs. Swenson were seated in the small room, and only Miss Conklin smiled at her.

"Yes, Mollie, come in. Oh, please get a chair from the kindergarten room next door."

Mollie brought back a chair, the one closest to the door so that she would not interrupt Mrs. Emmer's class. It was very low, meant for little children, and when she sat down, she felt like a five-year-old herself, surrounded by giants.

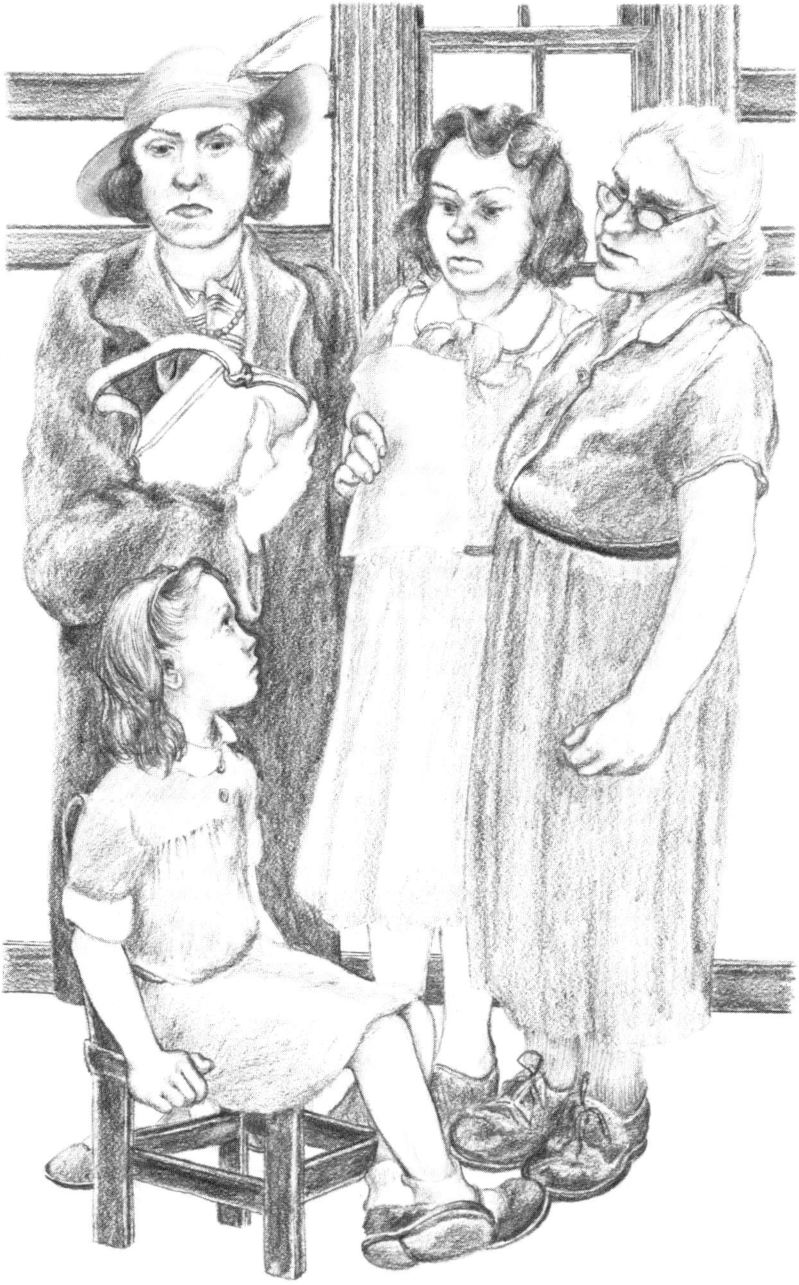

Miss Felt was holding a paper in her hand, gazing down at it every once in a while and then at Mollie. Mrs. Swenson, wearing a giant black hat with a green feather, did not take her eyes off Mollie for a moment.

"Do you know why you are here, Mollie?" Miss Conklin asked.

Mollie shook her head no, although she guessed it had to do with her make-believe brother.

"Is this the poem you submitted to the contest?" She took the paper from Miss Felt and handed it to Mollie.

It had been several weeks since Mollie had seen her poem, and she had supposed that it was now in the hands of the judges. It was a shock to see it still here in Miss Conklin's office only five doors down from her classroom. It had not gotten very far.

"Yes, that's my poem."

"It's quite a nice poem, Mollie," Miss Conklin said, still smiling. "Where did you find it?"

"Find it? In my head, I guess."

"Oh, come now," Mrs. Swenson said angrily. "It is perfectly obvious you did not make it up. Do you know what plagiarism is?"

"Some kind of sickness?" Mollie guessed, wondering what that had to do with her poem.

"No, Mollie," Miss Conklin said. "Plagiarism is stealing someone else's writing and claiming that it is your own."

"Which is not beyond this child," Mrs. Swenson said to the principal. "I have told you what a dishonest person she is. Dying brother and all that!" She looked at Mollie as she spoke. "Trying to make a fool of my daughter and me, humph!"

Miss Conklin pulled her eyeglasses halfway down her nose and looked over the rims at Mrs. Swenson. Mollie noticed that it was the same look she gave to students who didn't cover their schoolbooks. Then she slid her glasses back up again and turned to Mollie.

"Now, Mollie, we can understand how anxious you must

have been to win the contest. Not only for the money, I'm sure, but for the honor of simply winning," Miss Conklin said slowly. "Now, I'm sure you didn't understand the seriousness of what you were doing. Isn't that right?"

"But, I didn't . . ." Mollie began.

"There she goes again. Another lie!" Mrs. Swenson said.

"I'm not lying! I wrote the poem all by myself." Mollie felt a hot anger rising in her chest and tears coming to her eyes. "Don't cry in front of Mrs. Swenson," she told herself. She wiped her nose on her sleeve and sniffed.

"I'll tell you what we have in mind, Mollie. So far, Miss Felt has been unable to find the original source of your poem, but if you can prove to us that you did write it, we shall give it back to the judges for consideration. There isn't much time, of course, so you will have to hurry."

"I don't think she deserves any such chance," Mrs. Swenson said. "After all, I told you . . ."

"Yes, I know what you told me, Mrs. Swenson, but nevertheless, I think Mollie deserves the chance to prove to us that she did nothing dishonest."

Mollie waited, hunched up on the little chair, to hear what else Miss Conklin had to say.

"What we would like you to do is write another poem for us. Miss Felt will give you the subject, and if we can see that the quality of writing is the same, we will re-enter your poem. Now, how does that seem to you?"

"What do I have to write about?"

"Oh, I'll give you several topics when we get back to class," Miss Felt said. Mollie could see she wanted very much to believe that one of her students had written such a fine poem, but she was afraid of Mrs. Swenson.

"Until next week Wednesday I think should be time enough. That will be all, Mollie," Miss Conklin said. "Oh, take the chair back on your way out." Again she smiled. "Thank you, Mrs. Swenson, for bringing all this to my attention," Mollie heard her say as she walked back to her classroom.

CHAPTER *Thirteen*

Everyone had been curious when she returned to class after seeing Miss Conklin. Shelley passed her several notes, which Mollie ignored, and on the way home had tried to find out why she had been called into the principal's office. Mollie mumbled something about school. When Shelley continued to ask, Mollie said, "It's none of your business. Butt out."

When her mother came home, Mollie wanted to talk to her, but Mrs. Stone sent her to the store for a loaf of bread.

"You're very quiet this afternoon," Mrs. Stone said when Mollie handed her the bread and some change.

"Mom, did you ever get sent . . . ?"

"Only twelve cents' change? What happened to the other dime?"

Mollie dug into her pocket. No dime. "I don't know. Mom, did you ever . . ."

"Now, just a minute, young lady. Ten cents may be unimportant to you. You do nothing to earn money. Now, where is that other dime?" Her mother stood, hands on hips, and waited.

Mollie thought for a moment, then said, "Oh, yeah." She bent down, took off her shoe, and found the dime in the toe. "Here. I put it there so I wouldn't lose it."

"I was sure bread had not gone up that much," her mother said. "Now, what did you want?"

"I got sent down to the principal's office today." Mollie waited for her mother to get angry. She enjoyed when her mother became angry and then found out there was no reason to and had to apologize—like with the dime.

"Why? What did you do?" her mother asked much too calmly to satisfy Mollie.

"Oh, I didn't do anything, but they said I did."

"Who said?"

"Oh, them."

Now her mother was beginning to sound annoyed. "Who is 'them'? Mollie, will you answer me with a complete sentence? Now, why were you sent to the principal's office?"

"Because I wrote this poem and they said I didn't, and now I have to write another one to prove that I wrote the first one."

"Mollie, I have no time for nonsense. Now, what are you talking about?"

Mollie took a deep breath. "Well, you see, the school, or maybe the city—I don't know which—is having a contest for the best poem, and I wrote one, and the teacher and Miss Conklin—no, I don't think Miss Conklin, but Mrs. Swenson, yeah, she was the real one—said that I stole it from somewhere . . ."

"They accused you of plagiarism?"

"That's the exact word. How did you know that word?" Mollie was impressed.

Mrs. Stone sat down and began to pay careful attention. "Mollie, did they accuse you of plagiarism?"

"Yep."

"Mollie, did you steal the poem from someone else?"

"Mother!"

"Well?"

"No, no, I wrote it all by myself. Honest. If you don't believe me . . ." Mollie was sorry now that she hadn't shown them the poem when it was first written. There was nobody she could produce now to prove her honesty.

"To tell you the truth, I do believe you. I happened to come across that notebook while I was cleaning your messy drawers. What do you call it? *The Silver Songs* or something?" Her mother looked a little embarrassed, and Mollie was sure she knew the correct name, *The Golden Poems of Mollie Stone.*

Immediately, Mollie forgave her mother for snooping and breathed a deep sigh of relief. "I'm glad you found it, I suppose."

"But what did Mrs. Swenson have to do with all this?"

In her great relief, Mollie forgot to be careful. "Oh, she found out about the lies . . ."

"The lies? What lies?"

"Oh, remember when I went there for lunch and you got that note about Danny?"

"I thought there was something more to it than what you told me." Her mother was beginning to look angry again.

"Well, she was making fun of you because you worked, and I said . . ." Mollie told her the whole story about the brother with a glandular condition—and how the class whispered about Mignon and made her sick.

For a moment Mrs. Stone looked confused. She bit her lower lip and wrinkled her eyebrows. "Well," she said finally, "after that, I can understand how someone would think you were dishonest and capable of stealing."

"She's on *their* side," Mollie thought to herself. "I never should have told her."

"On the other hand," her mother continued, "that snobbish Mrs. Swenson has an awful lot of nerve picking on a little girl."

Mollie was surprised. She didn't know her mother thought of her as a little girl. It made her feel warm and happy inside.

"If Daddy isn't too tired when he comes home, I want you to tell him this story."

Mr. Stone was tired, but Mollie told him the story, anyway.

"What are you going to do?" he asked her.

"I guess I'll just write another poem and prove to those old . . ."

"No, you are not!" her father said. Everyone looked at him; he didn't raise his voice very often. "Mollie, you say you are innocent. I believe you. Your mother believes you . . ."

"I don't believe her," Danny said.

Mr. Stone ignored him. "Do you know what our laws say, Mollie?"

"Which laws?"

"The laws that govern our courts, the judicial system."

"Well, they say . . ." Mollie didn't really know.

"The law says that a person is innocent until proven guilty, and it is not up to you to prove your innocence. It is up to Mrs. What's-her-name to prove you guilty."

"Oh, listen, Ben, she's only a child," Mrs. Stone said.

"Does that mean she has no rights under the law?" Mr. Stone asked.

"But, Daddy, I'm not under the law. This is only for school," Mollie pleaded.

"Nevertheless, I feel that if your teachers, or whoever they are, don't believe you, they should have to prove that you are a plagiarist. Let them find the poem which you allegedly stole." Mr. Stone folded his arms and looked less tired than when he came home.

"But, I won't mind writing another poem, honestly."

"Absolutely no," Mr. Stone said. "And if there are any problems about it, I will take the day off from my office and go to school."

"No, no!" Mollie shrieked. The only fathers who came to school were big men in overalls whose arms were tattooed, the fathers of boys who said bad things to the teachers and were left back.

"I am going to write a letter to Miss Conklin on my legal stationery and tell her just what I've told you," Mr. Stone said. "Then we'll see."

Mollie's insides churned around. Why was her father making such a big thing about this? She thought he loved her, and now he was going to embarrass her to death. Not only that, he would make her lose the contest and the money for the bike.

"You're not being fair!" she screamed and ran to her room.

"Mollie, Mollie, come back. I only want to help you," her father called after her, but she slammed the bedroom door. "I wish they were dead, I wish they were all dead," she said to herself.

CHAPTER *Fourteen*

Mollie woke with a feeling that something uncomfortable had happened. But it wasn't until she looked in the mirror while combing her hair that she remembered what it was. Slowly she put down the comb and went into her parents' bedroom. She had wished them dead, and surely they must be lying there, still and pale. But the beds were empty and neatly made as usual.

"Gone!" she said to herself, "just as if nothing had happened."

Well, she would go, too. She would pack a suitcase and run away, never to be heard from again. They would all come home that day and find her gone, no trace. Should she leave them a note, Mollie wondered, No, let them worry. As a matter of fact, she decided, they would probably never even notice she was missing. And if they did, her mother would surely say, "Well, Frances, our new relative, is coming tomorrow, so it will all even out."

On the other hand, it would be exciting if they cried, if they called the police, if they ran up and down the block calling her name, if her father would say, "Oh, it's all my fault. I should not have been so mean." Or her mother would say, "No, it's my fault. I should not have gone to work today. I should have stayed home and made breakfast for my poor little girl whom I have been so cruel to."

The idea made Mollie sad. She sniffed and tried to make tears come. She looked around the room at her unmade bed, at the first-grade desk, at the window that looked onto the street. She decided to make her bed so her mother would not be angry, only sad.

Friday, Mollie remembered. She put on her blue skirt and white middy blouse; the navy scarf to wear around her neck was not in her drawer. "I suppose she didn't have time to iron it, again," Mollie said. "Oh, well, it doesn't matter. I'll never be at the assembly anyway."

She went downstairs and looked at the clock over the kitchen sink. Plenty of time. She would have something to eat. Oh, not a real breakfast, just some toast and jam and cocoa.

There was a note on the kitchen table propped up against the sugar bowl and an envelope.

"Ah," thought Mollie, "they're telling me they're sorry. Maybe I'll forgive them." She picked up the note and read it.

"Mollie, when you get home from school today, please go to Herman, the tailor, and pick up Daddy's blue suit. Money in envelope. DON'T FORGET CHANGE!" There was a dollar in the envelope.

"Oh boy, what a note!" Mollie said aloud. She bit off several pieces of toast, noticing that crumbs were dropping on the floor. She didn't care.

Leaving her plate and cup on the table instead of washing them, Mollie waved her hand to the kitchen cabinets. "Good-bye, all. You will never see me again."

Without thinking, she picked up her school books and bumped into Shelley, who was just coming in the back door.

"I'm early," Shelley said as Mollie looked at her in surprise. "My mother gave me cold cereal instead of hot. It didn't take me so long to eat because I didn't have to blow it to make it cool. It was already cool."

78

"You know something, Shelley, you're a dope." Mollie sighed.

They walked slowly because they were early, Mollie thinking all the while how to escape. She had made up her mind to run away, and now she was determined to go. Suddenly she doubled up as if in pain.

"Ow, ow," Mollie moaned.

Shelley stopped. "Whatsamatter? You sick?"

"My stomach, it hurts really bad, ow, ow."

"Go to the school nurse. She'll give you something," Shelley suggested.

"No, I can't walk that far." Still doubled over, Mollie turned around toward her house. "I'll see you later, Shelley, if I'm still alive. If I die, you can have my blue pencil case with the picture of the Indian on it. I will it to you." Clutching her school books with one hand and her stomach with the other, Mollie moved away. "Farewell, Shelley, remember me kindly."

When she was out of Shelley's sight, Mollie stood up and ran.

CHAPTER *Fifteen*

At the corner of her street, Mollie stopped running. Why was she going home, she wondered. She should be going toward Charlotte Avenue and the bus stop. She felt in her skirt pocket for the envelope with the dollar. It was still there. Looking around to see if anyone noticed, Mollie walked past her house and down toward Charlotte Avenue. A small group of people waited at the corner for the bus—luckily, nobody she knew.

"Where shall I go, anyway?" Mollie wondered. She really had not thought out this running-away business. She should have a plan, somewhere to go. "Oh," she decided, "I'll go to Boston to Aunt Ruth. I'll trade myself for Anna. Then Anna can come here to be with her sister Frances, and I will live with Aunt Ruth." Mollie was pleased with the idea and felt excited as the bus drew to the curb.

"Put a nickel in the box, kid," the driver said.

Mollie handed him the dollar to change. "How far can I go? I mean does this bus go to the railroad station?"

"Last stop, kid," the driver said.

Mollie plunked herself down on a seat near a window. She watched the familiar streets disappear. The buildings became taller and the streets more crowded as they neared the center of the city.

"I'm running away, I'm really running away," she

thought. Actually, this was not exactly as she pictured people running away. Most of the time, they had little bags tied to the end of sticks and walked through fields and over mountains where there were no houses. She remembered seeing a movie where a boy with a mean stepfather ran far away to an old aunt. She had made him take a bath and change his clothes, but otherwise she had been very kind.

"Last stop," the driver called. "Everybody out."

Mollie picked up her books and got off. She stood on the sidewalk trying to remember where the station was. Walking with her eyes on the buildings, she tripped over something. She looked down at a big bundle of dirty clothes.

"Watch where ya goin, kid," the bundle of clothes said.

Mollie gasped and jumped back. She had fallen over a person! He was just lying there in the middle of the sidewalk. "I'm . . . I'm sorry," she said.

"Got any money, kid? I ain't had a bite to eat since last Thursday," the bundle of clothes said.

"Yesterday or a week ago yesterday?" Mollie asked stupidly.

"What difference does it make, kid? Got anything for a poor old fellow who hasn't worked in more'n a year?" Red eyes gleamed up from the sidewalk.

Suddenly Mollie felt her arm being pulled. "Come away from him," a voice said, and Mollie turned. A strange woman, dressed very neatly with a fur collar wrapped around her neck, pulled Mollie toward her. "He's dirty —don't bother with him. He's a lazy old bum, a beggar!"

Then the woman turned to the bundle of clothes. "Don't you dare bother this child, you beggar! Get a job and don't bother decent people." The woman finally let Mollie's arm go and bent to whisper in her ear, "They blame it on the Depression," she said, "but they're all good for nothings, always were, always will be. It's disgusting! Go to the soup kitchen!" she called to the man, then

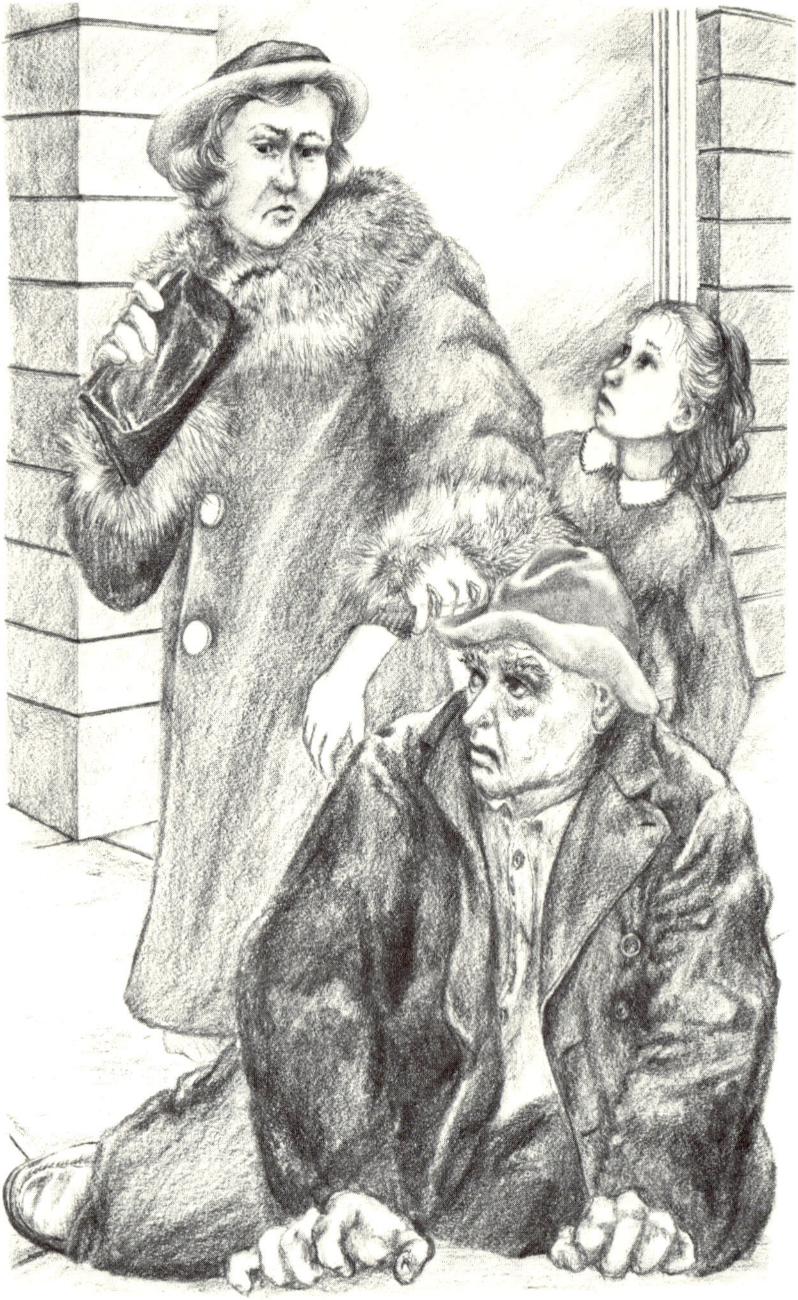

turned and walked away, leaving Mollie staring after her.

The bundle of clothes turned over and suddenly stood up, although Mollie could see he was not very steady on his feet. "They're to blame," he hissed to Mollie, "people like that. Just 'cause they were lucky and had a little something stored away, they think everybody else is a bum." His voice changed as Mollie started to move away from him, "Hey, come back, kid. I wouldn't hurt ya. Why I used to own a canny store, gave kids free licorice alla time." He was following Mollie but staying a little way behind so that no one would notice. "They took it away," he said louder. "Afta twenny years, they took it away 'cause I couldn't pay my bills." He seemed to be crying, and Mollie turned around to look at him.

"Aw, I don't want your money, kid. I mean I don't go aroun' askin' kids for a handout. I thought you was someone grown up."

Mollie turned to the man. "What's a soup kitchen?"

"A soup kitchen? Ain't you lucky you don't know! It's a place where they give you free grub. You stan' in line with a bunch of other poor coots who ain't got no job or no money, and these ladies give you some soup an' sometimes a piece of bread."

"Why don't you go there if you're hungry?" Mollie asked.

"Ta tell ya the truth, kid, I ain't really hungry. I mean I just et at one of 'em kitchens aroun' the corner there." He pointed a few blocks down.

"Then . . ." Mollie began.

"I know you're gonna laugh when I tell ya this, kid. Now, what would ya do if I came up ta ya or ta any of these guys passin' by and I said to you, 'Hey, could you give me some money 'cause . . .' You're gonna laugh, I know it. '. . . 'cause I wanna buy a necktie.' What would you do?" He didn't wait for Mollie's answer. "You'd tell me to get lost, right? I mean what's so important about a necktie, right?" The man suddenly straightened himself up, rubbed his scrubby beard, and brushed off his jacket. "But a necktie would make me feel real good. Better than a meal in a fancy restaurant. It would make me feel like shavin' and washin' my face and that I had a little"— he shrugged his shoulders—"a little dignity."

The word sounded so strange coming from the man that Mollie began to laugh.

"O.K., laugh, I knew you would. But let me tell you something, kid. A man can go hungry and thirsty and live in a shack, but he can be all right if"—he paused for a second—"if they let him keep his dignity. If they don't call him a bum or a liar!"

Mollie gasped. "They think I'm a liar," she said softly.

"That why you're runnin' away?" the man asked, just as softly.

Mollie didn't answer. "Could you get a necktie for"— she felt the coins in her pocket—"for thirty-five cents?"

"Yeah, a real nice one with stripes down the front. I used to have one like that." He looked into the air as if to see the tie floating there. Then he cleared his throat. "But I don't want your money. You go home and tell them you're a good girl, that you're not a liar, and don't let them get away with nothin'." He began to walk away, and out of the corner of her eye Mollie could see the bus coming into the station.

"Hey, mister, wait!"

But he was moving away. Quickly she ran for the bus, and as she ran, she dropped a quarter and a dime out of her pocket onto the sidewalk. The man turned at the jingle of the coins, and Mollie saw him bend to pick them up as she boarded the bus. He rose slowly, looked at her as she sat down inside the bus, and waved. "You're a good girl," he called. "Some day, when I get back my canny store, I'm gonna give you all the free licorice you want."

The bus pulled out and started back toward Charlotte Avenue.

CHAPTER Sixteen

The house was very quiet when Mollie walked in. It had begun to rain, and the living room was dark and gloomy, even though it was not quite noon. She wanted to turn on a light, but her mother had told her never to do that during the day. "Electricity is expensive and so are light bulbs."

Mollie sat on the sofa listening to the rain and wondering how she could fill the rest of the day. She wondered, too, what she could say to her parents when they found out she had played hookey.

Well, she decided, it was all their fault, anyway. If they hadn't butted in, if she hadn't told them, if they hadn't taken away her . . . her dignity. (She wondered which tie the man had bought for the thirty-five cents.)

If, if. She felt terrible—sad, angry, and a little afraid. It was like the time she had had to stay home with her brother at night, the first time her parents had left her alone—just she and Danny at night, all by themselves. There were noises in the house, creakings like someone walking in the cellar, moaning that came from Danny's room where he lay asleep. Was he being murdered?

She had sat on this sofa, huddled in a corner, watching the newspaper on the table. She was sure some invisible hand was turning the pages, for they moved, waved up, then back, page one, page two, as if someone were reading first one page and then the other. A breeze brushed her cheek. Had she opened the window? Or had someone else, outside?

Mollie had been afraid to turn around and look. What if she saw a face staring in at her, a face with big grinning teeth and hair all over it? Footsteps! Upstairs! Not Danny's, Mollie had been sure. Heavy footsteps that thumped suddenly.

And then a crash! Mollie had screamed and run upstairs. Silence.

With her heart beating so loudly she could almost hear it, Mollie had crept from room to room. Something in her father's closet or someone!

With one swift movement she had flung open the closet door, and a hundred wild things had hit her in the face. She gasped and covered her face with her hands. She waited, but nothing more happened.

Slowly she uncovered her eyes. The things were still there, flapping back and forth as the closet door swung slowly to a stop. Then Mollie had laughed with great relief. Her father's ties, hanging on the inside of the closet door, had fluttered in her face as she had flung open the door. And the crash had only been Danny in his nightly fall out of bed.

Mollie felt silly and stupid, but she had stayed awake until her parents came home.

The memory of that night and the ties made Mollie think of today and the one striped tie that the man wanted. Mollie wondered who "they" were who had taken away his candy store and his dignity.

When she had told the man that "they" had called her a liar, she knew exactly who "they" were—Mrs. Swenson and the others. But who could be strong enough to make a man lose his store and turn him into that sad, dirty person she had met? Mollie guessed it was the same "they" who had made the farmers' children in the movies so skinny and

86

wide-eyed and who made Frances and Anna's father jump out the window and her own father's clients unable to pay him his fees.

Mollie wondered about all this unhappiness in the world. It made her problem seem very unimportant.

She went up the stairs to her room and sat for a long time at her little desk, thinking and staring out the window. Then, she took her notebook of *Golden Poems* and began writing.

Mollie's back hurt, and she realized that she had been asleep at her desk. She jumped up, washed her face in the bathroom, and combed her hair, snapping the gold barrette tight around a clump of hair.

The rain had stopped as suddenly as it began, and she raced down to Herman, the tailor, relieved to find that the charge was only thirty cents for her father's suit. When her mother asked for the rest of the change, she would tell her she used it for milk money in school. For the next month, Mollie realized, she would have to wash her lunch down with water from the hall drinking fountain.

But, what should she do about playing hookey, Mollie wondered, as she stuffed the coins in her pocket. One of her parents would have to write a note or Miss Felt would not let her into class tomorrow.

"I know," she said aloud, "I'll tell the truth. I got sick on the way to school. Shelley saw me, even."

"What did you say, girlie?" Herman asked, turning off the pressing machine.

Mollie looked at him in surprise. "I said I got sick on the way to school."

Herman shook his head wisely. "Flu," he said. "It's the season."

Mollie gave a little cough in case there was any doubt.

CHAPTER *Seventeen*

From the doorway of the tailor shop, Mollie could see a new sign on the window of Higgins' Toy Shop.

"Maybe it's a sale," she thought happily. "Maybe my bike is reduced to five dollars . . . or three . . . or even one!" She walked as quickly as she could almost dragging her father's neatly pressed suit along the sidewalk.

But there were no bright letters announcing a sale. Instead, in carefully printed black crayon on a piece of cardboard were the words, "OUT OF BUSINESS." The door was locked with a heavy chain across it, and worse than that, the window was completely empty—not a doll, a ball, or a bicycle in sight.

Mollie couldn't believe it. Higgins' Toy Shop, where she had bought all her balls, all her jump ropes, where her parents had bought her first doll and carriage and a tiny red three-wheeler that she didn't remember, but Danny did. "Good-bye, rusty-fendered bike," Mollie whispered to the empty store.

She walked home slowly. What was the world coming to when candy stores and toy stores were going out of business? What would all the children do for jawbreakers and bubble gum and skates and stuff? Boy, grownups were mean, she decided, doing this terrible thing to the children of the world! A man passed by in his car, and Mollie stuck her tongue out at him. "Your fault!" she shouted.

"Fresh kids around here," the man said loud enough for Mollie to hear.

As she passed Shelley's house, the odor of baking came through the open front door and followed Mollie almost to her own front steps. She hung her father's suit in his closet and went downstairs for some graham crackers. Whatever Shelley's mother was baking had made Mollie very hungry.

"You feeling O.K.?" came Shelley's voice from the back porch. "You hardly missed anything in school today. I should of had a stomach-ache, too. You coming over to Florette's for the rehearsal? Hey, Mollie, you in there?"

"Yeah, I'm in here. Come in."

Shelley appeared, carrying a large sheet of paper, which she held out to Mollie. "Here's my part. I say, 'Ladies and Gentlemen, welcome to . . .'"

"Who cares?" Mollie said, taking a whole graham cracker in her mouth. "Ah on thin ah uh nets."

"What did you say?"

Mollie swallowed the cracker and washed it down with some milk. "I said I can't be in the show. Someone is coming tomorrow."

"Who? Someone I know?"

"No, you don't know her."

"Gosh, Florette and Elaine will be mad if you don't come. They'll have to change the whole program around, and it won't be much of a show if only four people— five, counting me—are in it."

"Well, let them be mad. I never wanted to be in their dopey show, anyhow."

"It's going to be on Florette's porch. They're going to open the windows wide so that you can hear Mignon play the piano in the living room."

89

"They can keep them shut tight for all I care. Who wants to hear fat Mignon play 'The Jolly Farmer'?"

"No, it says here on my announcer sheet that she's playing Ratch . . . Ratch . . . maneenoff's 'Prelood' in C Sharp Minor."

"Big deal."

"Oh, come on, Mollie. It'll be fun."

"I still have a sort of stomach-ache."

"Boy, I can believe you with eating a whole box of graham crackers!" Shelley said. "Well, if you feel better later, come over. And bring your poem." Shelley pulled out a pencil from a pocket. "Let me write down the name for my announcing. What is it?"

"Uh, it's called 'I Saw a Horse in Mignon's House Wearing a Skirt and Peasant Blouse.'"

Shelley started to write, then looked up. "Oh, come on," she said, giggling.

CHAPTER *Eighteen*

Mollie sat on the back-porch steps feeling tight and uncomfortable in her yellow party dress with all those ribbons on the sleeves. She hated the dress; it was too long as usual because her mother didn't get around to shortening it. She hated her cousin Rhoda for being so much taller, even though Rhoda had every right to be. After all, Rhoda was two years and fifteen days older than she. All her cousin's hand-me-downs were too long and frilly-silly like this one.

She hated her mother for making her wear it, and especially she hated Frances because her arrival was the reason for getting dressed up.

"We must make her feel welcome," her mother had said that morning, "because we're happy she's coming."

Mollie knew her mother was a little worried about Frances's coming to live with them. She had seen her adding long columns of numbers on a list marked "New Budget for Five," and sighing and crossing out and filling in.

The idea of sharing her room didn't please Mollie very much, either. She would probably be unable to read in bed if Frances wanted to sleep. She had already been forced to empty one of her dresser drawers and crowd her underwear and sweaters together in one. The same thing with the closet.

91

Not only that, but her mother would probably like Frances better because she was practically an orphan. "Better than her own child," Mollie thought miserably.

And, worst of all, her mother had decided that she would be able to work nights at the hospital if Frances were around "to mind the children."

"The additional money I'll make will pay for Frances's extra costs," Mrs. Stone had explained.

Now Mollie would hardly ever see her mother—maybe on a weekend or two she would show up and say, "My, Mollie, how you have grown!" or, "Your face is familiar, child, but I can't seem to remember your name."

Mr. and Mrs. Stone were down at the station this very minute, waiting for the train to come in, the train that would bring *her* to live in Mollie's house.

She spit on her finger and rubbed the saliva into her black patent leather shoes. They were beginning to get tight, but she loved them, the shininess, the little pearl buttons that held the strap over her foot. The bottoms were still practically clean because Mollie didn't wear them too much, only on special occasions.

"At one dollar and seventy-nine cents, they'll have to last a long time," her mother had said when she bought them.

A car door slammed, then another. Her father's voice could be heard from the front of the house. "He probably loves her better than me already," Mollie thought, although she knew that could never be.

"Mollie, where are you?" her mother's voice called. "We have someone who wants to meet you."

Mollie sighed and stood up. Slowly she marched through the kitchen and dining room, and there before her, clutching a brown shopping bag in one hand and a book in the other, stood Frances.

She was tiny, like a bird, Mollie thought. She looked to be about ten years old until you looked at her face. The big eyes were sad and had black shadows under them. And the mouth turned down at the corners as if Frances were about to burst out crying.

Instead, Frances smiled, a tiny smile that matched her body, and held out one hand, the hand with the book in it. "I bought you a present. Your Aunt Ruth says you're very smart and you like to read, so I bought you a book."

"Uh, thanks, uh, Frances." Mollie took the book and looked down at the title. *Leaves of Grass* by Walt Whitman.

"Oh, how thoughtful you are, Frances," Mrs. Stone said. "You shouldn't have done it, though. I know that books are very expensive."

"Not this one," Mollie wanted to say as she opened it. Stamped inside were the words, "Property of the Boston Public Library." Quickly she closed it. Stolen property! Well, probably poor Frances didn't know any better. And she was in another state, so they wouldn't catch her, anyway.

"It's really nice, Frances," Mollie said, feeling much better. "Come on upstairs, and I'll show you where our room is."

Frances looked at Mrs. Stone to see if it was all right. "Go right ahead, Frances. Unpack and then we'll have some lunch."

"Unpack!" Mollie thought, looking at the brown shopping bag that was bulging. Then she turned red. At the very top, where everyone on the train must have seen it, where her father must have seen it and Danny who had just come into the house must have seen it, on the very top was a pair of white underpants!

Mollie grabbed the bag. "Come on, Frances. I'll show you where we sleep."

Silently Frances followed. She let out a happy sigh when she saw Mollie's room. "Oh, it's beautiful!" Mollie looked at her. She had never thought of her room as beautiful.

Two maple beds with overwashed chenille bedspreads, a dresser and mirror, and the first-grade desk and chair. Mollie had always wanted one of those flowery fat chairs to sit in that she had seen advertised in the newspapers, but she knew that it was too expensive. The walls had been papered when they moved in, when Mollie was very small, and had pictures of red and blue balloons floating all over it, some faded to pale pink.

"You can have this drawer," Mollie said, opening the bottom drawer of the dresser, "and half of the closet." She looked doubtfully at the brown shopping bag. "Is that all you have?"

"Yes," Frances said, looking out the window. "You have a nice quiet street outside."

As if it were a signal, the nice quiet street burst into shouts.

"Mollie, come on, we're waiting, the show is about to begin," Shelley was calling.

Then a whistle, a boy's whistle that required two fingers stuck in the mouth, which Mollie had tried to do but couldn't. Herbert.

Mollie leaned out of the window. She could see other kids in twos and threes marching toward Florette's house. Florette's brother was at the door collecting admission—a penny, they had decided, was fair.

"I have company. I can't come."

"You have to," Shelley whined.

"Oh, yes. Don't bother about me. I'm fine. Go to your friends," Frances said.

"Oh, it's only a dumb show," Mollie said.

"A show? You mean you sing and dance? Oh, I'd like to see that."

"I don't sing and dance," Mollie said, with some annoyance. "I am the world's greatest poem reciter. I write my own, too."

"You coming?" Shelley called.

"Oh, O.K., in a minute." She turned to Frances. "Wanna come?"

"Well, I have to see if your mother needs me for anything. I am supposed to help her, you know."

"Oh, she won't mind. I mean she said you were supposed to be a sort of relative. We're not supposed to treat you like a servant."

Frances looked at Mollie for a long time. "That's very kind."

"I have some dopey friends. Oh, a couple are all right, but most of them are"—Mollie made a circle around her ear with her fingers—"you know, screwy, nuts."

"Don't say that, Mollie. You have no idea what . . . what screwy, nuts is like," Frances said seriously.

Mollie blushed. She had forgotten that Frances's mother was in a hospital for crazy people. "I didn't mean . . ."

"Oh, it's all right," Frances said, but she sniffed as if to hold back her tears.

"Hey, listen," Mollie said. "I don't have to go."

"Yes, go. Maybe I'll come over after lunch."

"Well, O.K." Mollie hadn't wanted to go, but now she didn't want to stay with Frances who had all these problems that would make Mollie afraid to say anything. Hoping Frances could not see what she was doing, Mollie opened the dresser drawer, removed *The Golden Poems*, and found the one she had written on the day she had run away. Then, with a wave of her hand, she went down the stairs two at a time and ran across the street to Florette's.

A broom had been stuck upside down into a flower pot filled with sand. This was the microphone, Shelley explained. An assortment of bridge chairs, canvas beach chairs, and boxes were for the audience of about a dozen kids in the little backyard. Shelley was sitting on a porch step studying her script, and Herbert was hanging from a tree by his knees. There was no sign of the Songbirds or Mignon, but there was surely the sound of them.

"Do re me fa sol la ti do," sang Elaine from somewhere inside the house. The piano banged and tinkled. The audience was whispering and waiting expectantly with the exception of a tiny red-haired boy who kept yelling for his mother. Mollie surveyed them from the steps, the poem folded and sticky in her palm.

"Sit here," Shelley said, pointing to a stool in the corner. "Boy, you're sure dressed up. Except your dress is too long."

"It's the new style." Mollie gave her a mean look and plunked onto the stool, her legs stretched full length before her.

"Ps-ss-t, begin," Elaine hissed from the window. "Mollie, poke Shelley."

Mollie kicked Shelley lightly without moving from the stool. "They're ready."

Shelley stood up, smoothed her dress, and cleared her throat. "Ladies and gentlemen, welcome to the Beautiful Hour of Entertainment. First on our program is Herbert Hartz telling jokes."

Herbert jumped down from the tree. He stood behind the broom-microphone, grabbed the handle, and began. "One guy says to another, 'Hey, do you know why a disease should wear a girdle?' The other guy says, 'No, why should a disease wear a girdle?' The first guy says, 'So the germs won't spread.' Ha ha, that's a good one."

The audience giggled, not at the joke, Mollie guessed, but because he had said girdle. Anyway, that was why she giggled.

Herbert told three more jokes, all with the same two guys in them. The audience laughed and applauded, and Herbert went back to his tree.

Shelley then introduced Mignon playing her "Preelood," and the sound of the piano was heard faintly through the open window. The audience became restless as the piece went on and on. Even Mollie yawned in the warm afternoon sunlight. The dress was beginning to stick

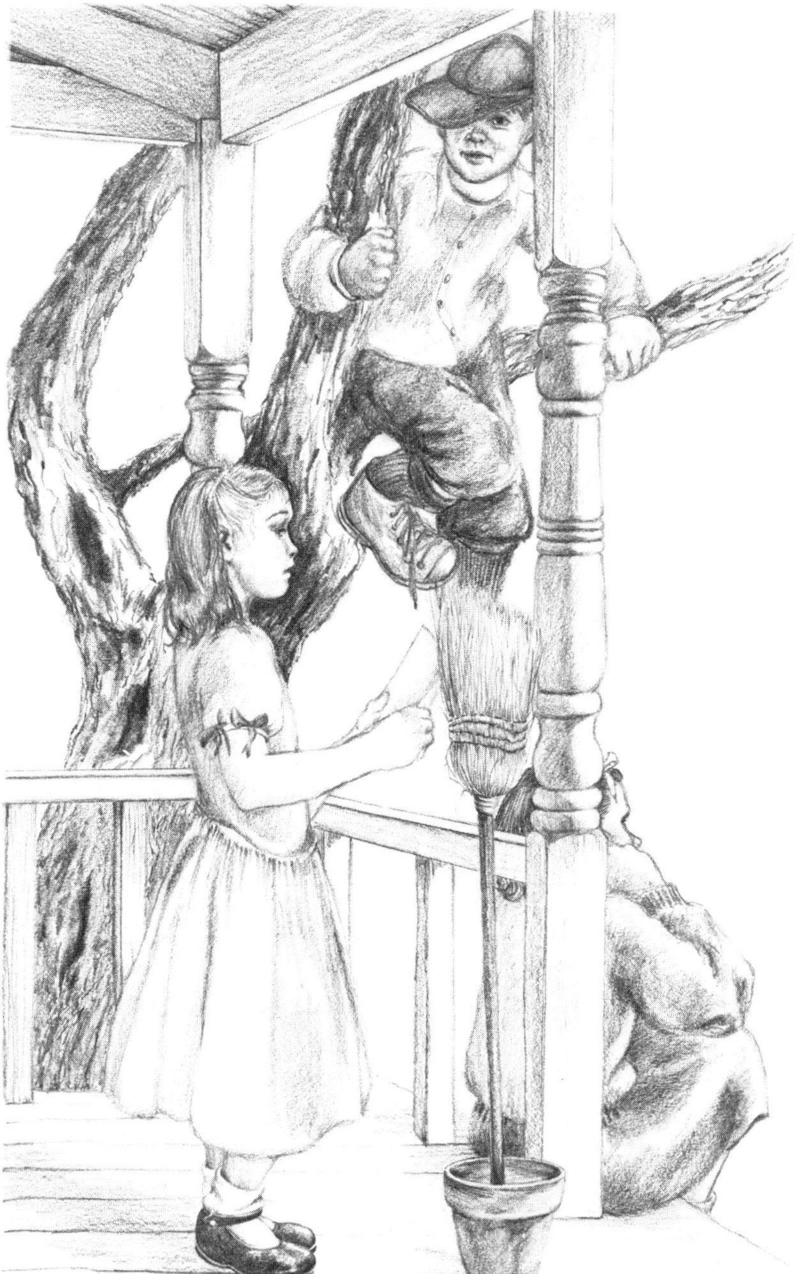

to her, and she wiped her forehead with the yellow frilled skirt.

"You're next," Shelley whispered.

Mollie didn't use the broom. She stood next to it and in a loud voice said, " 'They' by Mollie Stone." She cleared her throat and read from the wrinkled paper:

> "I wonder who the people are
> Who cause the sadness on this earth.
> In country near and country far
> *They* steal the happy smiles and mirth.
>
> "*They* take away, *They* rob and cheat,
> *They* call you names so hard and cruel,
> *They* make you poor and life unsweet,
> *They* send you begging for some gruel.
>
> "One or twice, I've met some *They*.
> So have we all, you will agree,
> Who tore your heart, and stole your pay,
> Your work, your home, your dignity."

Mollie stared at the audience who was also staring at her. There was a sprinkling of applause and then some very loud clapping in the rear. Mollie looked up. Her father and Frances were clapping their hands together as loudly as they could. "Bravo," her father yelled. "That's my girl."

Mollie gasped and ran back to her stool. Mignon was leaning against the porch railing, smiling at Mollie.

"There goes the porch. Mignon's standing on it," Mollie said to Shelley.

"I don't care what you say about me," Mignon said slowly. "I know you're only joking. That was a good poem, Mollie. Can I borrow it to show my mother?"

"It's my only copy," Mollie said, but she handed the paper to Mignon. She couldn't wait for the Songbirds to finish their duet. She just wanted to get out of there.

CHAPTER *Nineteen*

On Monday morning, Mollie found a bowl of unlumpy hot cereal waiting when she came downstairs. Frances was standing there, pouring freshly squeezed orange juice into a glass. Mollie's school books were tied together neatly with an old strap from a broken roller skate. There were some flowers in the blue Shirley Temple pitcher on the table.

"Gee, you didn't have to do this, Frances. Don't you have to go to school?"

Frances laughed. "I like to help a poet, such a good one, too. And, no, Mollie, I don't go to school anymore. I'm too old."

"Too old? I thought you were about fourteen."

"No, Mollie. I'm nineteen."

"Nineteen! Gee, this is like having a big sister." Mollie sat down and enjoyed her hot cereal, which nearly burned her tongue.

"Tomorrow, and from now on, Danny will walk to school with you. I can get him off in the morning, so your mother won't have to rush. Won't that be nice?"

"You can't have everything," Mollie said with a sigh. But Frances's company in the morning and after school was pretty nice, she decided. Danny's presence was not too much to pay for it.

"Who was that?" Shelley asked as they walked to school.

"My cousin. She's staying with us for a while," Mollie said happily.

In the schoolyard, Miss Felt came over to the girls as they waited for the bell to ring. "Mollie, may I see you privately?" She took Mollie by the arm. "Miss Conklin asked me to tell you that everything is all right. Somehow"—she winked at Mollie who stared at her in surprise—"Miss Conklin and Mrs. Swenson are convinced that you wrote the contest poem. Isn't that nice?"

"My father wasn't here, was he?" Mollie asked. "I mean he didn't come to school, did he?"

"Your father? Why no, he didn't. Why should he?"

"Oh, nothing. I just thought maybe . . ."

"I'll tell you something else, Mollie, but don't tell a soul, promise?"

Mollie shook her head. Miss Felt was awfully friendly all of a sudden. "They're making the announcement a week from Friday at assembly. Isn't that exciting?"

Mollie shrugged. "I guess so." What good was the contest now, Mollie asked herself. The bike was gone forever, and she would never find it even if she won the money.

Miss Felt waved and the bell rang.

"I just figured it out," Shelley whispered as they walked into the classroom. "Only two more weeks till school ends. Yippee!"

At dinner that evening, only her father, Danny, Frances, and she were at the table. Mrs. Stone was working late. Frances had fixed a delicious supper.

"Steak?" Mr. Stone asked. "Sort of expensive, isn't it, Frances?"

"No, they had a sale. Mollie, tell your father the good news."

"Hey yeah, Miss Conklin believes me. She said I didn't have to prove anything about the poem."

"Grand, Mollie, grand. They dropped the plagiarism charges, did they? The old battle-axes!" He laughed, and so did everyone else.

"I'll do the dishes, Mollie," Frances said as Mollie began to clear the table. "You go do your homework."

Upstairs on her little desk, Mollie found a bright silver fountain pen tied in a note that read, "To a Nice Girl."

She whooped down the stairs and threw her arms around her father. "Thanks, Dad, it's beautiful."

Her father looked at the pen. "Yes, it certainly is, but don't thank me. I didn't give it to you."

"You didn't? I thought maybe one of your clients went bankrupt and paid you in fountain pens."

"One of my clients went bankrupt, but he didn't pay me in fountain pens," her father said, laughing.

"Well then . . ."

"Oh, you like the pen?" Frances said. "It's from me."

Mr. Stone looked at the pen, then at Frances. "You? But, Frances, that's a very expensive pen."

"Well, it was my mother's, but she doesn't need it any more."

"That's very nice of you, my dear," Mr. Stone said. "Mollie, take very good care of it."

"Oh, I will, and thanks a lot. Boy, your mother's pen." Mollie took it up to her room and examined it closely. It didn't look old. It was in very good condition, as a matter of fact. She filled it from her inkwell that was built into the little desk. As she unscrewed the cap, she saw a paper sticker. On it was the price of the pen, three dollars, and the name of the jewelry store on Charlotte Avenue.

Mollie tried to put the thought out of her mind but couldn't. Her new cousin, Frances, the orphan from Boston, was a thief.

If she told her father, what would he do? Send her away, probably. That would mean the end of hot breakfasts and someone to talk to and someone to do the dishes.

Maybe she should mention it to Frances, Mollie wondered, sort of hint. But then, what if Frances would cry and, worse yet, what if Frances would say she didn't do it? Well, there was that library book by Walt Whitman to prove something.

"I'll return the pen to the jewelry store," Mollie thought. But how? They would want to know where she got it. They would think she was the crook who had decided to go straight at last, as Edward G. Robinson said in the movies.

Well, she wouldn't use it, Mollie decided, and put the pen in her little desk drawer.

CHAPTER Twenty

There were no more gifts during the week, and the family had no more steak for dinner.

"She's given up her life of crime," Mollie thought happily. "Frances has gone straight."

Now, she would not have to report her, and she would just forget about the pen till "it cooled over," as Edward G. Robinson said in the movies.

"You know, Shell," Mollie said as they walked home from school that Friday, "the movies are really true to life. I mean they say a lot of true things in them. You want to go tomorrow? They're playing the final chapter of Flash Gordon where he finally gets Ming the Merciless, Ruler of Mongo."

"If it doesn't start too early. You know, tomorrow's the day."

"What day?"

Shelley looked surprised. "You know, tomorrow morning, 10 A.M. . . . ." Shelley began to sing. "Good morning, little friends of mine. Hope that you're all feeling fine . . ."

Mollie remembered. "Oh yeah, tomorrow morning the Songbirds are gonna be on Uncle Pat's show."

"What are you going to wear?" Shelley asked, but didn't wait for Mollie's answer. "I'm wearing my blue dress with the lace collar."

"For what?"

"To listen to the show."

"You mean you're getting all dressed up to sit in your living room to hear the show?"

"No, in my bedroom. I have a radio in my bedroom, too. My father can't stand them, so I have to listen in my bedroom."

"That's dumb." Mollie laughed.

"Well, after all, they are my best friends."

Mollie tried not to look hurt, but she was. "I thought I was your best friend."

"Well, you are, of course, but Florette and Elaine, well, you know."

"Oh yeah, well, I suppose, they're my best friends, too." Mollie began to feel mean. "I mean I've known them at least a year longer than you have because we moved here before you. And"—Mollie paused for the importance of the next statement—"because Florette is related to my mother's cousin. She's probably *my* cousin for all I know."

"She is not. You're just making that up."

"Yeah, well if you don't believe me, ask Florette. It so happens that her Uncle Morris is related to my mother's cousin Sylvia." Mollie's father had once mentioned something like that, Mollie remembered.

"You know, I think I'll just wear my old shorts. I mean, after all, in my own bedroom it would be kind of silly to get dressed up," Shelley said.

"I'll probably be in my pajamas. I won't even wear my bathrobe," Mollie declared.

"I may not even turn on the radio." Shelley was determined to go Mollie one better.

Mollie felt a sudden power. Shelley was so easy to tease.

But, of course, everyone on Laurel Avenue, and probably Uncle Morris and Cousin Sylvia, whoever they were, turned on the radio Saturday morning. Even Mrs. Stone, who was showing Frances how to polish the furniture, stopped. "Mollie, put on a bathrobe," she said.

"I'm all dressed," Danny said. "See, Mom?"

"Sh-h," Mollie hissed. "You'll make me miss them."

"Ah, he's only talking about some corn flakes. Mom, can I have some corn flakes?"

Mollie knew her brother was jabbering just to annoy her. She gave him a hard pinch.

"Ow, she pinched me. Mom, Mollie pinched me," he wailed.

"Then just be quiet," Mollie shouted. "Ooh, we missed something. What did he say, what did he say?"

"He said," Mr. Stone replied, walking into the living room, "that if you want to be big and strong like Uncle Pat, you must eat your Corny Corn Flakes."

"Oh, good," Mollie said, "we didn't miss them. Hey, he's saying it, he's saying their names."

And he was. And there they were. Like two sick cats on the back fence, Florette and Elaine wailed their way through a song about how deep was the ocean and how high was the sky. The audience applauded, and it was all over.

"Boy, that was terrible," Mollie said, disappointed that it was over so quickly.

"I liked it," Danny said, just to disagree with his sister.

"I wonder if Anna heard them," Frances said. "Do they get this program in Boston? If Anna and I heard the same thing at the same time, it would be as though we were in the same room."

Mrs. Stone looked at Frances. "You really miss your sister, don't you?"

"Oh, I know she is happy with Aunt Ruth and Uncle Arthur."

Mollie studied Frances's face. Was she serious? Did she really miss her sister? "Boy, I wouldn't mind if he was a thousand miles away," Mollie said, pointing to Danny.

105

"Don't say that, Mollie. You don't know what you're talking about," Frances said.

"Hey, Mom, can I have ten cents?" Mollie changed the subject.

"Flash Gordon is going to capture Ming the Merciless, Ruler of Mongo, in about half an hour at the Laurel Theater."

CHAPTER *Twenty-one*

There was no doubt about it. He was a policeman and he was standing at the front door and Frances was crying. Mollie, Shelley, and Danny stared at him as they came in the back door from school.

"You'll have to wait. There will be no one here to take care of the children if I go."

"That the children?" the policeman asked, pointing over Frances's head. "They look as though they can take care of themselves for a while."

"What is it? What's happening, Frances?" Mollie asked, although she was sure she knew.

"I have to go to jail." Frances burst out crying. "He says I stole some things."

"I think I'll go home now," Shelley said, darting past the policeman. "I'll see you later."

Mollie knew that in a few minutes everyone in town, probably the whole world, would know about Frances. Shelley was the world's greatest blabbermouth.

Danny, too, began to cry. "No, no, don't take her away," he screamed, clutching Frances's skirt.

"Can you wait a minute, officer?" That was what her mother called the policeman who once stopped her for going through a red light. "I want to call my father."

"Well, you can call him, but I can't wait. Tell him I've

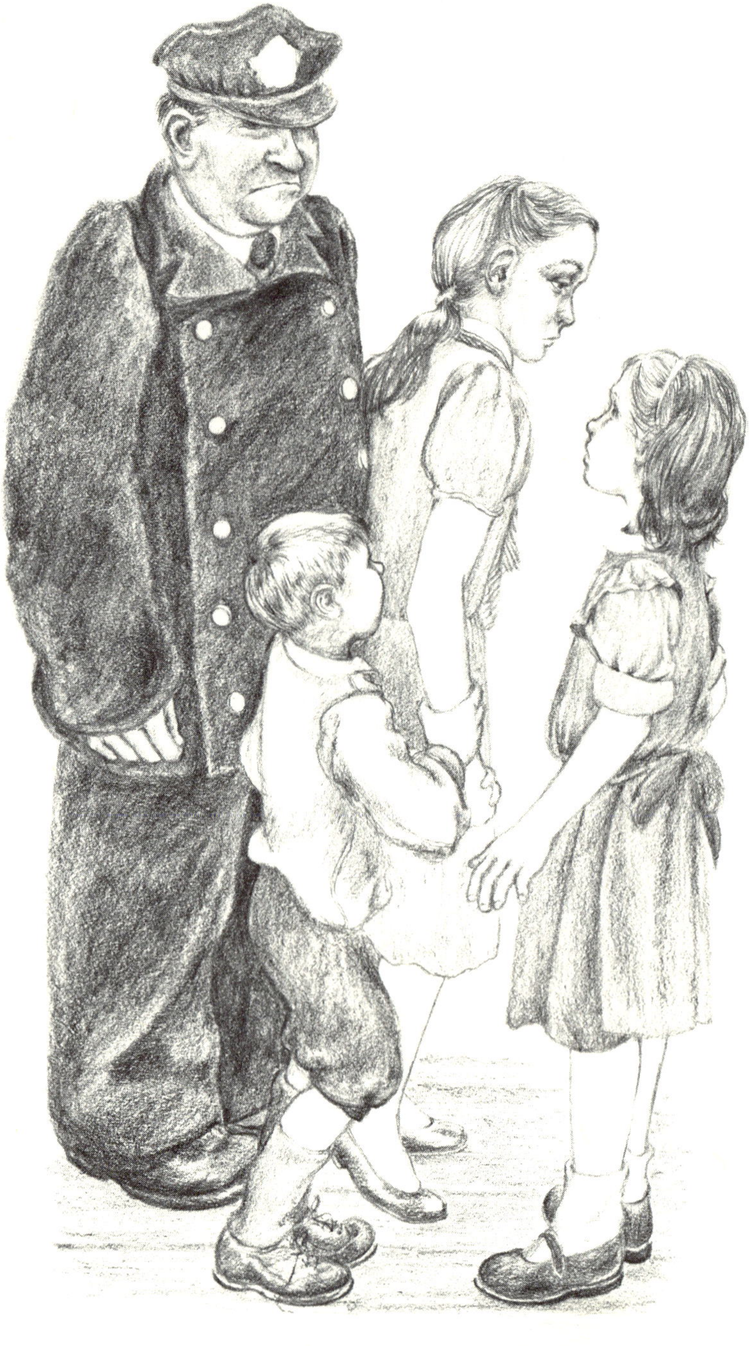

taken the prisoner to the Rosedale station house. Come on, Miss, let's go."

Danny was screaming, Frances was sobbing, and Mollie was shaking. But she managed to call her father at his office. She told him what had happened.

"I won't come home—I'll go to the station house and find out what this is all about," he said, and hung up.

Mollie and Danny sat together on the living room sofa for what seemed like ten years, but it was only an hour later when Mrs. Stone walked in.

"Oh, Mom, you'll never believe it," Mollie began.

"Yes, I will. Someone told me at the hospital. She heard it from someone else who heard it from Mrs. Weller. Bad news certainly travels fast."

"Mrs. Weller! Shelley's mother! Boy, she's as gabby as Shelley," Mollie said angrily.

"Mollie set the table. I don't know whether Frances will be home tonight."

Frances did not come home. Mr. Stone walked in looking tired and unhappy. "Well, they've really got the goods on her. Two stores made the complaints, a jewelry store and a butcher. The butcher says he actually saw her leave with a whole chicken under her coat."

"The pen," Mollie said.

"Yes, the pen and a ring she wanted to send her sister. A piece of junk actually, but I guess that doesn't matter."

Nobody was very hungry.

"Can I go see her?" Mollie asked.

"No, she'll be there for a few days. The trial is Wednesday. I don't know how I'm going to defend her, but I'll try my hardest," Mr. Stone said.

"You're a good lawyer," Mrs. Stone said. "It's the world that's so awful."

Mollie agreed. "*They* have done it again," she said.

CHAPTER *Twenty-two*

The trial was at four o'clock. Her father had given Mollie permission to be there, and she raced to the courthouse, which was about a mile from the school and which Mollie had never seen before.

Her mother had taken the afternoon off from the hospital, even though it meant losing the seventy-five cents an hour she was paid. Mollie was surprised to see Florette and her mother there, too.

"Well, they know Aunt Ruth. Our cousin Sylvia is related to someone in Florette's family," Mrs. Stone explained.

"Uncle Morris," Mollie informed her mother.

There were other people there, too, sitting on the hard benches behind some kind of fence that separated the judge's platform from the spectators. They were all strangers to Mollie, who asked her mother why they were there.

"Frances is not the only one being tried. There are others, and I suppose these people are relatives or something."

Her mother was right. Four men were brought in separately, two nicely dressed, one old man, and one who looked as if he never bathed. There was a lot of mumbling in front of the judge, which nobody could hear, and Mollie was getting restless.

"When does Frances come?" she asked.

Before her mother could answer, Frances appeared from a door behind the judge, and Mr. Stone was with her. Frances looked awful. Her eyes were swollen, and her dress was a drab gray that Mollie had never seen in her closet. But her father looked very handsome. The sunlight made the gray in his hair look silvery. He was wearing the blue suit Mollie had brought home from the cleaner and a bright red tie.

"Your husband looks so dignified," Mrs. Sherman, Florette's mother, whispered.

Mrs. Stone looked very proud. Mollie wanted to run up and hug him.

More mumbling, a loud rap from the judge's gavel, and then Mollie's father began to speak.

"Your Honor, this may be an unimportant case for the courts—petty larceny is the charge, a charge that involves only a small amount of money. But you undoubtedly realize that this case is very important to the young lady standing accused before you.

"When Frances came into our home, all of her belongings fit into a brown shopping bag. That isn't much to show for nineteen years on this earth. We tried to make her feel welcome. We hoped that she would realize that she was a part of our family, for that is how we thought of her. But still, Your Honor, this young woman felt that she was taking from us without being able to give anything in return. She did not see herself as being a great help to my wife and a friend to my children. She did not know that these things were the giving of herself, which is far more precious than gifts or money. But, Your Honor, what happens to a person who feels that she owes, that she is in someone's debt, that she is a charity case—even though we never, never thought of her in this way?"

"I once thought she would be our servant," Mollie thought guiltily.

Her father continued. "There was not one item that was stolen that she kept for herself. Everything was for us, a way to say thank you. That is, except for the ring she wanted for her sister, a ring to say 'Remember me. Even though we are separated, I am still thinking of you.' Who do these children have except each other? Their father dead, their mother desperately ill and unable to care for them. Giving made Frances feel like an equal. It gave her a certain amount of dignity in the eyes of those she wanted to please—or so she thought."

"Dignity again," Mollie thought, remembering the ragged man she had met.

"If you put this girl in prison, what will it gain? She knows she has done wrong. She has punished herself enough with her remorse. She has been punished enough by society already. I will personally guarantee that this young woman, the defendant, will not break the law again. Let's not put one more crime on the conscience of our society. We have hurt her enough. I beg you to give her another chance."

The judge nodded. Mollie held her breath, hoping he would speak loud enough so that she could hear. Her father had said everything so wonderfully. How could the judge put Frances in jail?

Mr. Stone was wiping his forehead, waiting for the judge to speak. He put his arm around Frances, who looked at him with love.

The judge cleared his throat. He did not put Frances in jail. He said that she could go, but that she would have to report to the court every month for one year and tell them how she was getting along.

"Yes, yes, Your Honor, thank you, Your honor. I will be very good. I promise." Shyly she kissed Mr. Stone on the cheek as they walked through the fence.

Mollie and Mrs. Stone stood up. So did Florette and her mother.

"If only Elaine could have been here," Florette whispered to Mollie, "she would have had such a good time crying."

"Yeah," Mollie said, blowing her nose hard.

CHAPTER *Twenty-three*

Tomorrow was the last day of school. It was also the day of the Friday assembly when the announcements would be made about the contest. There was no homework because all the books had been taken away, and Mollie loved the feeling of walking home from school with no load to carry.

She stood over the piano wondering what to do. She banged a tune that was really more noise than music.

"I'm gonna tell Momma you're banging the piano," Danny said, sneaking up behind her. He tickled the keys at the high end of the keyboard. "See? You must be gentle, like me."

Mollie whirled around, put her chin on her chest, and raised her arms high, letting her fingers hang down. "Ming the Merciless is going to kill you." She walked slowly toward her brother, knees stiff. "The Ruler of Mongo is going to pull out each finger, each fingernail, ha ha ha."

"Ha ha yourself," Danny said and walked out.

She couldn't even scare her own brother any more. The world was surely coming to an end. Mollie went into the dining room and stared at the mirror above the sideboard. She narrowed her eyes, crossed them, made strange shapes with her mouth, and pulled out her barrette and mussed her hair until it stood out like a brown haystack in a field.

"Beautiful," someone said behind her.

Mollie whirled around. "Oh, it's you," she said to Florette and Elaine. "Don't you knock at the house of the Mad Monster?"

"We did. Your brother let us in. Obviously you were too busy making faces to hear us." The Songbirds giggled.

Mollie shrugged her shoulders. "Want a graham cracker? We're out of jelly, so we're using blood."

"No thanks. Is your father home?" They smiled at each other.

"My father? What do you want with him?"

"Our parents want to talk to him."

Mollie's mind raced over all the possibilities. Why did they want her father? Was Florette's brother in trouble? Did she do something wrong?

"He's not home yet. He had to go to court today to save a client who threatened to stuff Uncle Pat into a corn-flake box."

The girls didn't seem to hear her. They were taking turns in front of the mirror, smoothing their hair and trying out new smiles. "It's very important," Florette said at last.

"Well, I'm his private secretary at home." Mollie picked up the pad near the telephone and a pencil. "You may give me any messages, and if I like them, I shall give them to Mr. Stone," Mollie said in her imitation of Miss Felt's British accent. "What is it you want, my dears?"

"Tell him to come to Florette's tonight, please. We have some important business to discuss."

"Yeah, I'll just bet," Mollie said with a sneer.

"O.K.," Elaine said, putting her hands on her hips and tossing her Tootsie Roll curls, "if you don't believe us, we'll get another lawyer."

"Wait a minute. You mean you want him to be your lawyer?" Mollie was very confused.

"The light dawns," Elaine said to Florette. "Isn't she brilliant?"

"Why?" Mollie asked. "Did you murder somebody with your singing? Is your father going bankrupt?"

"You know," Elaine said, again to Florette, "this person doesn't seem to understand there are other reasons for hiring a lawyer."

Florette nodded. "Just tell him, will you, Mollie? Come on, Elaine."

When her father came home that evening, Mollie gave him the message.

"What in heaven's name," he said. "I hope George isn't having any business problems." After dinner, he put on his hat, took his worn leather briefcase, and went to Florette's.

Mr. Stone was gone for over an hour. When he came back, both Mollie and her mother practically jumped at him. "What is it? What did they want?"

Mr. Stone smiled. "You won't believe it. I'm not sure that I believe it after hearing them Saturday morning."

"What? What?" Mollie screeched.

"Uncle Pat liked them so much, he's going to have them on regularly, to sing the Corny Corn Flakes song."

"Ooh," Mollie said, holding her nose. "Nobody will eat them."

"That's not the opinion of the radio people. They want them to sign a contract."

"You mean, they're using you for their attorney?" Mrs. Stone asked.

"Yes, they . . . or rather Florette and Mrs. Sherman . . . were very impressed with my defense of Frances. They told me I was a wonderful lawyer." Mr. Stone laughed as if to say some people were very strange.

"You are a good lawyer," Frances burst in. "You're the best in the whole world. They are very smart people to be using you for their contract."

"Is there much money involved?" Mrs. Stone asked.

"A goodly sum. As a matter of fact, the Songbirds will be making almost as much money in a week as I have in a long time." Mr. Stone scowled for a moment at the thought, then brightened. "But it was nice of them to think of me."

"Why not?" Mrs. Stone asked. "After all, we are practically relatives."

"You mean Morris and Sylvia? Well, that's the long way around." Mr. Stone laughed.

"Are we rich?" Danny asked.

"Rich! Far from it! But this will give me a very nice fee for the next six months at least."

Bicycles of every color rolled through Mollie's head: golden wheels, a bell that peals, any bike that I like.

". . . pay the electric bill, the coal company, and replace the muffler on the car," her mother was saying. "Mollie, what are you mumbling about? Did you do your homework?"

"Have none. Tomorrow's the last day of school, remember?"

Mrs. Stone groaned. "I hope you'll keep busy this summer," she said to Mollie.

"Oh, she will," Mr. Stone said mysteriously. "Don't worry about that, Edith."

CHAPTER *Twenty-four*

The very last day of school! The last assembly program until September! Just in time, too, because the day was very hot, and Mollie's starched white blouse and navy tie felt scratchy and sticky.

Miss Felt told the two biggest boys, Philip Sheridan and Herbert, to open the tall classroom windows with the long poles, but there seemed to be no breeze.

The teacher was fanning herself with a notebook and wiping her forehead every once in a while with a rag. It was the same rag that was used to wash the blackboard, and the front of Miss Felt's hair was powdery with chalk dust.

Mollie watched some perspiration roll down the back of Mignon's neck and waited for it to disappear into the creases of fat. She was so engrossed in the path it took, around this roll, down the next, that she didn't hear the ten o'clock assembly bell.

Mignon stood up, and Mollie's eyes followed her.

"We're waiting, Mollie," Miss Felt said with a sigh. "Are you planning to sit there all summer?"

Everyone giggled, and Mollie looked around to see them lined up in size places. She squeezed in between Shelley and Florette, and Miss Felt led them out the door. The hallway was a little cooler, but not much.

"Hot," Miss Felt said to another teacher. "I can't wait to leave for my sister's place in the mountains."

Mollie was surprised. She had never thought that Miss Felt was related to anybody, that she had a family and something to do when there were no more classes to teach. She waited for a few more clues to Miss Felt's other life.

"I bought one of those new two-piece bathing suits," Miss Felt was saying.

Shelley giggled. "A two-piece bathing suit! She's so old!"

"How old do you think she is?" Mollie asked Shelley. The fact that Miss Felt had birthdays was also hard to believe.

Shelley shrugged. " 'Bout twenty-five. Look how white her hair is in front."

"Move along, children, let's not dawdle," Miss Felt said, although she herself moved along the hallway very slowly.

In the auditorium, the same music as every Friday pounded from the piano, followed by the same greetings by Miss Conklin, who was saving her good-bye speech until the end.

Then, that man! This time, Mollie noticed, he had no hat and wore a light-colored suit, but she would have recognized him anywhere. Mr. Guss from the Brotherhood of Atlantis! Mrs. Swenson was on the stage, too, but she didn't get up from the folding chair that had been placed there by somebody.

Mr. Guss cleared his throat and began. Mollie could hardly hear him because of the noise her heart was making. Someone was standing up—a girl in the fourth grade. Mollie watched her walk to the stage, up the stairs, and stand looking straight out into the audience.

Mollie's heart beat slower. "I lost," she said to herself, "to a kid in the fourth grade!"

But␣Mr. Guss was holding up a picture full of bright flowers and a funny-looking rabbit with three ears.

"The painting contest," Mollie whispered to Shelley. "That kid won the painting contest."

"Only third prize," Shelley whispered back. "My mother knows her mother."

Mr. Guss was talking again, this time about the poetry contest.

"The third prize was awarded to a young man at P.S. 156 for a poem entitled 'The Snows of Christmas.'"

"Christmas always wins," Mollie whispered. She was sorry she hadn't written about Christmas.

". . . and the first prize went to a student at P.S. 78 for a poem entitled 'Halloween Ghosts,'" Mr. Guss announced. "But the second prize went to a student from right here at P.S. 135. . ."

"P.S. 132," Miss Conklin corrected loudly.

"I mean 132," Mr. Guss said, turning a little pink. "And here to make the award is the president of your Parent-Teacher Association, one of the judges, Mrs. Henrietta Swenson."

Mollie heard Florette whisper to Mignon, "That's your mother." Mignon gave her a strange look. Mollie had just about given up winning anything. And what did it matter now that the bike was gone? She slumped low into her seat! A poke in the ribs made her sit up straight. "It's you! Get up!" Shelley was hissing.

"What? Me? What for?"

"You won second prize. Go up to the stage," Florette whispered from the other side.

Miss Felt stopped fanning herself and was waving to Mollie. "What's wrong with you, child?" she said as Mollie slid past three pairs of boney knees. "I just knew it," the teacher whispered as Mollie passed her.

As if in a dream, Mollie found herself shaking hands with Mrs. Swenson, with Mr. Guss, and with Miss Conklin. She could hear Herbert's fingers-in-the-mouth whistle and Miss Conklin say not very angrily, "We'll have none of that whistling. Applause is quite enough."

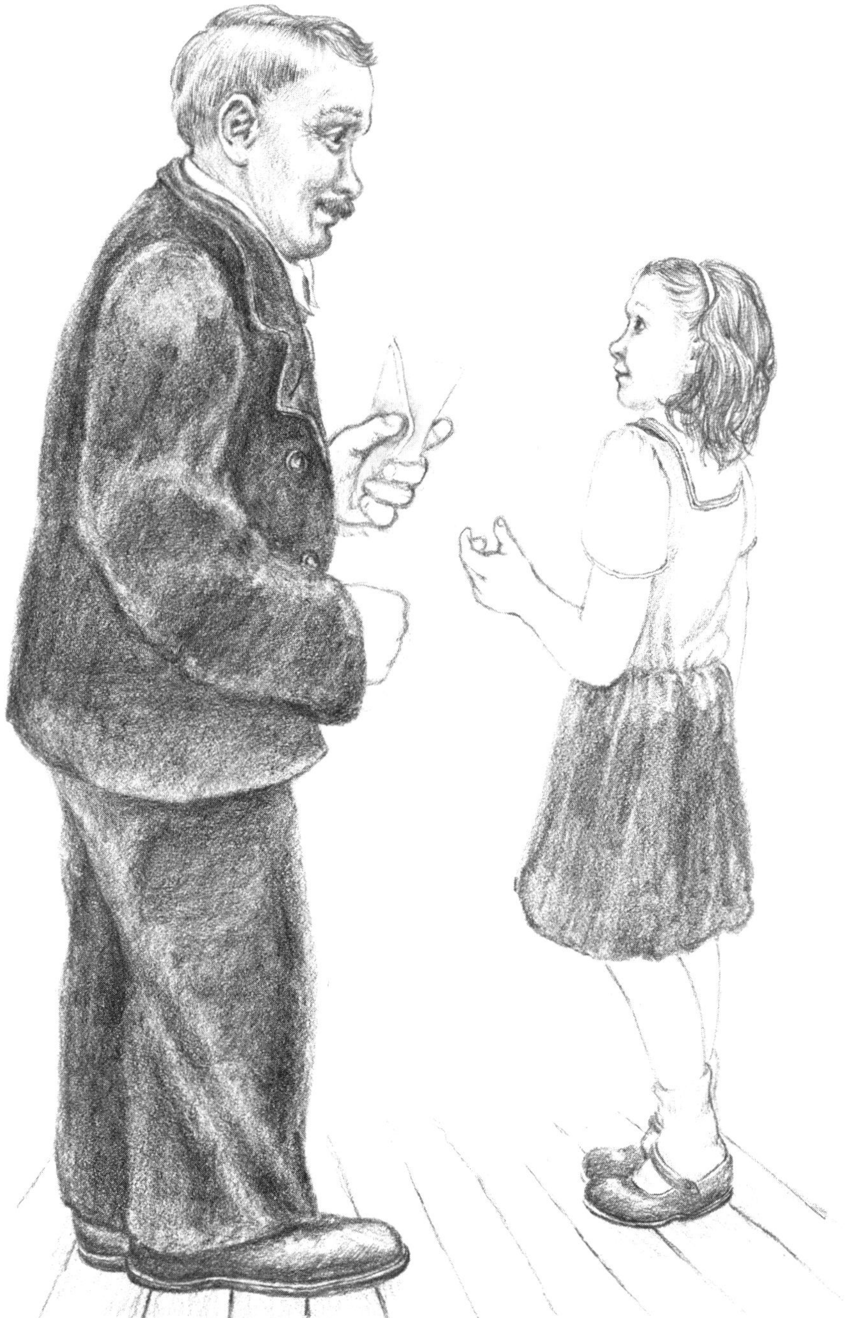

Then she was back in her seat, clutching an envelope with five one-dollar bills in it.

"Boy, are you lucky!" Shelley whispered.

"No luck," Mollie replied after everything calmed down inside of her. "Just brains, my dear." She had never thought of winning second prize, but now, considering what Mr. Guss had announced—that two hundred students had entered the poetry contest—it was not bad, not bad at all.

Miss Conklin was saying farewell. "Have a lovely summer, children. See you in the fall." And the piano banged out the marching-from-assembly music.

CHAPTER *Twenty-five*

Big-mouth Danny had beat Mollie home with the news. Frances was waiting for her when she came in.

"Congratulations, Mollie," she said, hugging her. "Danny told me the wonderful news."

Mollie gave Danny a mean look. "Why did you have to do that? It was my poem and my prize. I wanted to tell."

"Well, you can tell your mother and father, Mollie. They're the most important. Danny, you won't say a word, will you?" Frances turned to Mollie's brother and shook her finger at him.

"Aw," Danny grumbled.

Mollie went up to her room, took out the five dollar bills from the envelope, and studied them. Her mother would have to work a whole day for that, she thought.

She sat on her bed, then rose and slipped the money into her notebook, *The Golden Poems of Mollie Stone*. She opened the book wider and read some of her work.

She shook her head as she read the lines. Once she thought they were so good. She wondered about the other winners. Did they think they were good, too? Then she put the notebook back under her sweaters and picked up the book Frances had given her. Mr. Stone had already sent the money to the Boston Public Library to replace it.

Now it was really a gift, if not from Frances, then from her father.

"Walt Whitman," Mollie read and then:

> "When lilacs last in the dooryard bloom'd,
>   And the great star early dropp'd in the western
>   sky in the night,
>   I mourn'd, and yet shall mourn with ever-
>   returning spring."

Mollie sighed. Would she ever be able to write like that? Would she ever be able to think such thoughts, although she was not quite sure what they meant? No, she was not really a poet, Mollie told herself, at least not yet.

She put the book back on her desk. "I'm not really a poet, and I don't have a bike," she thought gloomily, going downstairs and into the kitchen.

"Buy any more graham crackers?" she asked Frances.

"Your father's home," Frances said with a smile. "He's in the backyard."

"My father? So early?"

"Go and tell him your news," Frances urged.

"It's not really so important," Mollie said, searching in the pantry for the crackers.

"Go, anyway," Frances said, and laughed softly.

Her father was standing beneath the cherry tree, and he was polishing the reddest, shiniest bicycle Mollie had ever seen.

"For you," her father said, pointing to the bike.

Mollie stared and held her breath. She was dreaming. She had fallen asleep upstairs and was dreaming. Oh, it wasn't fair to have dreams like this.

"Poor Mr. Higgins," Mollie's father was saying as if through a mist. "This was all he could pay me for handling the bankruptcy." He pushed the bike toward Mollie.

Mollie moved forward. The metal handlebars were hot

in the afternoon sun. Her father rang the bell that was attached to the handlebars, and the jingle made Mollie jump.

"It's real, it's real," she cried.

"And all yours," her father said.

"But poor Mr. Higgins, he has no more store. What will he do?" She thought of the old candy store owner. "Will he have to go to the soup kitchens and beg for food?"

"No, he said he could do some bicycle repairing in his garage. Poor fellow, after all these years!" Mr. Stone sighed. "But that's the way of the world, Mollie, at least for the time being."

"It will get better, won't it, Daddy?" Mollie asked.

"It can't get much worse," he answered. "But thank God for what we have—each other and our health."

"And dignity. How was Mr. Higgins' dignity? Did he still have it?" Mollie touched the shiny handlebars and felt a little guilty about her good luck.

Mr. Stone looked at her curiously. "It's odd you should ask that, Mollie, because as we signed the last papers, Mr. Higgins said to me, 'I ran an honest business and I don't need charity, so I guess I still have my dignity.'"

Mollie felt much better about owning the bike.

"Yes," her father continued, "we've been very, very lucky."

"I know," Mollie said. But she could wait no longer. She jumped on the red shining bicycle and rode out of the yard, waving to her father. "I forgot to tell you," she called over her shoulder. "I won second prize."

Her father raised his clasped hands over his head like a victorious prizefighter, and Mollie noticed the glint of his silvery hair as she turned the corner of the house.